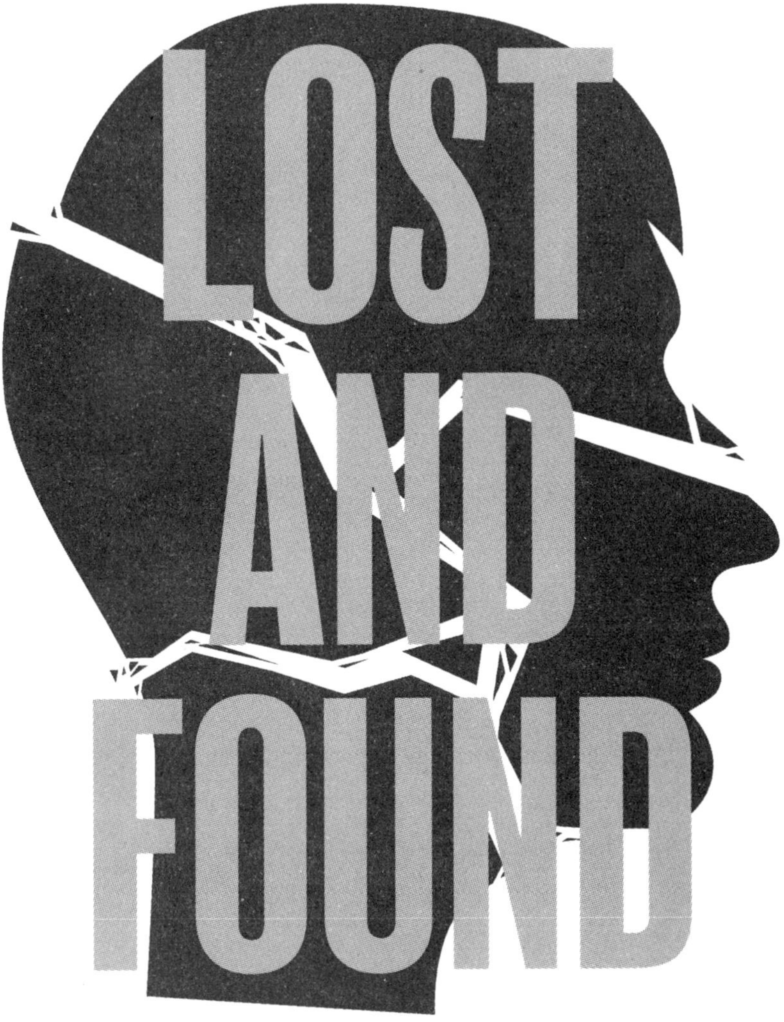
LOST
AND
FOUND

CONTENTS

CONTRIBUTORS

Sam Allberry is a speaker and apologist for Ravi Zacharias International Ministries as well as an editor with The Gospel Coalition. He is the author of *Is God Anti-Gay?* and *Seven Myths About Singleness*.

Quina Aragon is a spoken-word artist and author who lives in Tampa, Florida, with her husband and 3-year-old daughter. Her first children's book is *Love Made.*

Chris Castaldo (PhD, London School of Theology) serves as lead pastor of New Covenant Church in Naperville, Illinois. He is the author of several books, including *Talking with Catholics about the Gospel.*

Sam Chan is a public speaker for City Bible Forum, Australia. He is a global citizen—born in Hong Kong, studied medicine in Sydney, got his PhD from Chicago—who speaks to high schoolers, city workers, bankers, doctors, and lawyers. He loves helping people rediscover the joy that comes from faith, spirituality, and the Christian tradition.

Jason Cook is associate pastor of preaching at Fellowship Church in Memphis. He earned his MDiv from Beeson Divinity School in Birmingham, Alabama.

Collin Hansen is editorial director for The Gospel Coalition. He earned an MDiv at Trinity Evangelical Divinity School and an undergraduate degree in journalism and history from Northwestern University.

Bernard N. Howard is a Jewish believer in Jesus. He moved from Britain to New York City in 2012 and is the pastor of Good Shepherd Anglican Church, which he planted in 2017 with his wife, Betsy.

Aixa de López is a pastor's wife and mother of three girls and a boy. They live in Guatemala City. She writes, doodles, and speaks. She regularly blogs at http://www.aixadelopez.org.

Jeff Robinson is lead pastor of Christ Fellowship Church in Louisville, Kentucky, and senior editor for The Gospel Coalition.

Vaneetha Rendall Risner is the author of *The Scars That Have Shaped Me* and blogs at danceintherain.com, although she doesn't like rain and has no sense of rhythm. Vaneetha is married to Joel and has two daughters.

Joni Eareckson Tada, CEO of Joni and Friends International Disability Center, is a bestselling author and international advocate for people with disabilities. A diving accident in 1967 left Joni Eareckson, then 17, a quadriplegic in a wheelchair.

Christopher Yuan is a speaker and author of *Holy Sexuality and the Gospel*. He also co-authored a memoir with his mother, *Out of a Far Country: A Gay Son's Journey to God and a Broken Mother's Search for Hope*.

HAVE YOU MET JESUS?

——

BY COLLIN HANSEN

"I LEARNED THERE ARE MANY PATHS TO LOSE YOUR WAY. AND ONLY ONE WAY TO FIND IT."

Did you know life was going to be this hard? I must have missed all the school assemblies devoted to disappointment and failure. I don't remember any class on how to adult. At least sports were somewhat realistic. Neither the teams I rooted for nor the teams I played on experienced much success. More often than the thrill of victory I knew the agony of defeat. But ecstasy usually chased agony with a trip to McDonald's for french fries and a McFlurry. Ah, the wonders of an 18-year-old metabolism.

A little later on I recited the vows. Better or worse. Richer or poorer. In sickness and in health. But how was I supposed to know what any of this meant at 22 years old? You're too young to even understand you're poor. Sickness? At our age? That only happens in summer blockbusters young men are obligated to take their girlfriends to see.

When life seems worse than expected, we're told, "It gets better."

But what if it doesn't?

You need more than a cliché when real life dawns. Because life is hard. You don't always know what will get you. You just know something will. Addiction. Depression. Unemployment. Student loans. Rejection. For me the hardship came in threes, one after the other: I couldn't find a job. My wife and I couldn't conceive a child. We lost much of our savings in the Great Recession.

I didn't know if we were going to be okay. Nothing had been promised to me. Not the job I pursued after three years of additional graduate education. I left wonderful co-workers to follow what I thought to be God's call. But what did I have to show for it? I hadn't been promised a child, either. I wondered if my wife and I had waited too long. It seemed so easy for all our friends and family. They wanted a child, they got a child . . . or two or three or four. I wasn't promised financial security. We made the right decision to buy a house. Until it wasn't the right decision anymore. In fact it was the kind of decision you make at 23 that still haunts you at 33. And with student loans on top of it all, and no promise of a lucrative career, I didn't know how to provide for the kids we couldn't have.

I couldn't change my circumstances. And that was the hardest part for me. I'm a fixer. A planner. I had been taught as a child that if you work hard enough, you can reach your goals. And for the most part that advice proved true. When I worked hard, good things happened. Until they didn't. I had been responsible. I had been discerning. I had been diligent. No matter. The effect would have been the same if I had slacked off at work, binged on Netflix instead of studying, and gambled away my inheritance on those bad sports teams I still love.

What do you do next when your life's motto turns out to be a lie? If you're like me, first you turn to despair. I didn't handle things well. I was lost. And the more I looked inside myself for answers and solutions, the more frustrated I grew. I found no resolution. I found no peace. After all, I'm the one who got myself into this mess. Why did I think I could get out of it by the same way? I wasn't in control. And that was the hardest part of all for me to handle.

I learned there are many paths to lose your way. And only one way to find it.

MY SHEPHERD

Throughout this ordeal I knew myself to be a Christian. God had shocked me at age 15 with an experience of his grace. I wish I had the proper words to explain it to you. I just remember that one day I was a brooding teenager who didn't understand himself and didn't know how to fit in. And the next day I knew joy and belonging. I'm not sure at the time if I comprehended much more. At some level I finally felt the truth of what I had previously only been told: that Jesus loved me and had forgiven my sins, so I will live with him forever.

This conversion surprised me, because all I had known of church to this point was begrudging participation. I couldn't wait to graduate from church. I didn't understand the fuss. There are many good ways to spend your Sunday. Sleeping. Watching football. More sleeping. Unless this Christianity thing is real. But it sure didn't seem real to most of the folks I knew at church. Why bother with the charade of dressing up and dragging yourself out of the house to hear old songs and a short message of questionable relevance? Jesus might have risen from the dead on the third day. But we didn't know where to find him. Or bother to look very hard.

So it caught me, my friends, and my family off guard when suddenly I knew Jesus lived in my heart by faith (Eph. 3:17). And I was happy. That was the weirdest thing. I've always been known as a fairly serious person, even as a young child. It's not easy for me to make fast friends through small talk. Jesus, though, made me happy. I felt as though I had found myself and the way I was meant to be. The truth is that I had been lost in myself, but Jesus had come to find me.

In my church growing up we had a big, beautiful stained-glass window in the back. Jesus held a shepherd's rod in one hand and cradled a little lamb in the other. It's the kind of symbolism you take for granted if your earliest memories include the church. But it's understandably confusing if you're reading the Bible for the first time and wondering about all these seemingly outdated images of God as a shepherd. Probably the most famous example comes from Psalm 23:

> The LORD is my shepherd; I shall not want.
> He makes me lie down in green pastures.
> He leads me beside still waters.
> He restores my soul.
> He leads me in paths of righteousness
> for his name's sake.
>
> Even though I walk through the valley of the
> shadow of death,
> I will fear no evil,
> for you are with me;
> your rod and your staff,

they comfort me.

You prepare a table before me
in the presence of my enemies;
you anoint my head with oil;
my cup overflows.

We see here an image of a God who goes before his people and walks beside his people. The psalmist, David, understands God as an intimate companion, a reliable comfort. When Jesus arrives in human flesh in what we know as the New Testament, he picks up on this shepherd imagery of God. And he applies it to himself, as the good shepherd (John 10:11). But Jesus confuses the exact people who have been reading, reciting, and singing Psalm 23 their whole lives. You see, Jesus doesn't approve of the religious leaders. And they don't approve of him, because he prefers to hang out and eat with the sinners, the folks shunned by their polite religious society.

Jesus turns religious expectation on its head. The head of the line is actually the back. Only the lost will be found. Even the most insignificant person in the world's eyes matters infinitely to God. Jesus explained by telling the religious leaders this story:

What man of you, having a hundred sheep, if he has lost one of them, does not leave the ninety-nine in the open country, and go after the one that is lost, until he finds it? And when he has found it, he lays it on his shoulders, rejoicing. And when he comes home, he calls together his friends and his neighbors, saying to them, "Rejoice with me, for I have found my sheep that was lost." Just so, I tell you, there will be more joy in heaven over one sinner who repents than over ninety-nine righteous persons who need no repentance. (Luke 15:4–7)

Only the lost will be found. And the ninety-nine who don't realize they're lost will never find their way home to God.

AMAZING GRACE

I don't know whether you know Jesus or not. I don't know if you grew up in church or in another religion or in no religion at all. Whatever your background, I want to ask: Have you ever really met Jesus? Have you ever heard him speak in the pages of his Word? Do you know his good news, or do you only hear of him through his self-appointed spokesmen on cable news?

The Jesus of history—the Jesus who lives yesterday, today, and forever—might surprise you. He surprised everyone he met during his 30-some years walking among us. And no wonder. No one ever spoke like he did, then or now. He spoke with authority and yet also with the gentle touch of an intimate and sympathetic friend. He spoke with consistency, across the years and among different audiences. Our record of Jesus comes from witnesses who followed him for years. These witnesses believed in him, though they didn't always understand him. Not until his death on the cross, his resurrection on the third day, and his subsequent appearances among them did they begin to truly grasp his purpose, his message, his gospel. But once they learned, they never forgot. Once they realized they were lost, he found them.

Jesus taught his followers many things during three years of public ministry. But none of it really made sense until they emerged from the daze of disappointment during those dark days in the shadow of the cross. After his resurrection, Jesus helped his followers discover their true selves. It had been his plan all along. And that plan involved his own death. He told them:

> Truly, truly, I say to you, unless a grain of wheat falls into the earth and dies, it remains alone; but if it dies, it bears much fruit. Whoever loves his life loses it, and whoever hates his life in this world will keep it for eternal life. If anyone serves me, he must follow me; and where I am, there my servant will be also. If anyone serves me, the Father will honor him. (John 12:24–26)

By all appearances Jesus lost on the cross. His mission was thwarted. The religious leaders finally caught up to him. The Roman authorities added another notch to their gory, bloody belt. But Jesus tells us that's not the way of

God's kingdom. Death brings life. If you live only for today, you'll dread tomorrow.

You'd struggle to find any clearer teaching from Jesus, as confusing as he may seem to modern ears. Today we're told to find ourselves by looking within. We're told that love means accepting everyone else just as they are. But it doesn't work. Sometimes we don't do what we want to do. We hurt others. And they hurt us. We plan. And others thwart those plans. We rage against the evil of this world. And the evil seems to grow. What can break the cycle of hate?

"Whoever finds his life will lose it," Jesus tells us, "and whoever loses his life for my sake will find it" (Matt. 10:39).

What does he mean? Anyone can love someone who loves them back. Anyone can thank God when things are going well. But what would give you the power to love and even forgive and reconcile with someone who hurt you? What would cause you to feel thankfulness even when you don't get the promotion, when you don't get the scholarship, when you don't get the girl? The same power that led Jesus to cry out from the cross, "Father, forgive them, for they know not what they do" (Luke 23:34). Only the kingdom of God can help us find hope in a lost world. When we pick up that cross and follow him, we find the meaning of a life worth living.

"If anyone would come after me, let him deny himself and take up his cross and follow me," Jesus told his disciples. At this point he hadn't yet gone to the cross. So they didn't understand. But they never forgot. "For whoever would save his life will lose it, but whoever loses his life for my sake will find it" (Matt. 16:24–25).

You need good news that will sustain you even in your worst nightmare. When all your planning is for naught. When yet another pregnancy test is negative. When you don't know when the next paycheck will come. When you don't know how to pay the mortgage. When you look inside yourself for answers and emerge only with despair. When all the affirmation of the world can't help you love yourself. When the clichés of youth slip like sand through your fingers.

And you need this good news even more when everything's going well. When you get the girl. Land the job. Buy the vacation home. Because Jesus tells us that when you feel at home in this world, you won't enjoy the next.

"If anyone would come after me, let him deny himself and take up his cross and follow me," Jesus told a crowd. "For whoever would save his life will lose it, but whoever loses his life for my sake and the gospel's will save it. For what does it profit a man to gain the whole world and forfeit his life?'" (Mark 8:34–36; see also Luke 9:23–25).

In order to find your life, you must lose it for the sake of

Jesus. To discover your true self you must forsake this world. This book aims to help you understand and believe these words from Jesus. We want you to know how you can endure any hardship with faith and peace. We want you to see how love overcomes evil with good. We want to introduce you to the One who brings healing and hope and purpose to life. We want you to lose your life so that God would find you.

I've never found that life gets easier. Or better. But I have found that God is with me. That Jesus walks with me through the valley of the shadow of death. That he will leave the 99 in order to find me when I call out to him. That he promises me nothing in this world except that the God of the universe sees and knows and loves me, and that in the next world I will see him face to face, when he lifts the burden of my sin and the evil of this fallen world.

Once I was blind, but now I see. Once I was lost, but Jesus came and found me. Amazing grace, how sweet the sound! It saved a wretch like me.

CHAPTER 2

THE DEEPER HEALING IN CHRIST

BY JONI EARECKSON TADA

"FORGET THE SIN PART; I JUST WANTED THE HEALING PART."

For as long as I can remember, I was into sports. Whether racking up swimming medals, slamming a tennis ball with my wicked backhand, or being voted "best athlete" in my senior class, I had found my niche, my *life*. I was an athlete, and it defined everything about me, even the major I planned on declaring in college.

But athleticism can push a person too far. Only a month after high-school graduation, I broke my neck while attempting an inward pike dive off a raft in the shallows of the Chesapeake Bay. I had assumed I could pull out of the pike in time, but when my head crunched against the sandy bottom, my arms and legs went limp. When they pulled my paralyzed body on shore, I kept thinking, *What a stupid dive; why did I do it?* Months later, when the permanency of my paralysis began to sink in, I felt my life was over.

I was a Christian back then, but life in Christ didn't define who I was. True, I understood I was a new creation with a new heart, at least in theory, but I didn't act or even live like it. So, after my accident, I dug into my Bible for help, hoping that Jesus would give me back all that I'd lost. I wanted—I needed—my body back.

I scoured God's Word for any reference of Jesus healing paralyzed people. One passage caught my attention: Luke 5.

> Some men came carrying a paralyzed man on a mat and tried to take him into the house to lay him before Jesus. When they could not find a way to do this because of the crowd, they went up on the roof and lowered him on his mat through the tiles into the middle of the crowd, right in front of Jesus. . . . So, he said to the paralyzed man, "I tell you, get up, take your mat and go home." Immediately he stood up in front of them, took what he had been lying on and went home praising God.

That's all I read. I ignored the verses *within* the ellipsis (vv. 20–24) in which Jesus teaches that forgiving sin is a lot harder to do than healing someone. I bypassed the point of the passage, that Christ's authority to deal with sin gives him the right to deal with withered legs and arms. Jesus even infers that healing a paralyzed man is a piece of cake compared to purchasing that same man's redemption.

I didn't care about that teaching. Forget the sin part; I just wanted the healing part. As far as I was concerned, if I kept my nose clean and stayed out of trouble, Jesus would have no reason *not* to heal me.

And so, I made the rounds at local healing services, following every scriptural injunction that might qualify me for physical healing. Elders prayed and anointed me with oil, and I confessed more sins than I could recall. But after two visits to Kathryn Kuhlman's healing crusades (the Benny Hinn of her day), I plummeted into despair. My arms and legs remained unresponsive. Didn't God know I was lost without limbs that worked? Didn't he understand I was a strong athlete on the inside? Surely he knew I was the least likely candidate to enjoy life in a wheelchair.

After the third healing crusade, my sister drove me home to our Maryland farm. All the way, I kept fuming, *What kind of Savior, what kind of rescuer or healer, would refuse the prayer of a paralytic? Especially a paralytic who claims Christ as her Savior?* I felt bewildered and utterly lost. One morning I awoke early, looked around my shadowy bedroom, and decided I didn't want to get up. *If I can't be healed,* I thought, *then I'm just not going to do this. . . . I am not going to live this way!* I stayed in bed that day. And the next. And the following week.

Soon a bitter root—a real spirit of complaining—began to take hold. Nothing anybody did was good enough. Every hurdle I faced became a reason to feel sorry for myself. If I couldn't be healed, it was, *Just leave me in bed. Close the drapes and shut the door.*

The despair was claustrophobic, and I finally whimpered, "I can't live this way. I'm so lost. God, *show* me how to live." It was my first plea for help. Next came fresh days when my sister would get me up, plop a Bible on a music stand, and park my wheelchair in front of it. With a mouth stick, I would flip this way and that, trying to make sense of it all.

Of course, I was still interested in what the Bible had to say about healing. I found out in the first chapter of the Gospel of Mark. There, Jesus is performing all kinds of healings throughout the day and long past sunset. Next morning, the crowds return, and Simon and his companions search for Jesus. He's nowhere to be found—he had awakened early and gone off to a solitary place to pray. Finally, they find him and tell him about the crowd of diseased people at the bottom of the hill, all looking to be healed. But Jesus casually replies, "Let us go somewhere else—to the nearby villages—so I can preach there also. That is why I have come" (Mark 1:38). His words were stunning. Jesus walking away from diseased and disabled people who were looking for healing? People like me?

It struck me: It's not that Jesus didn't care about all those

"PHYSICAL HEALING PALED IN COMPARISON TO THE UNTHINKABLE ABUSE MY TRANSGRESSIONS HEAPED ON MY LORD."

people; it's just that their momentary problems weren't his focus—the gospel was. The good news that says, "Sin kills . . . hell is real . . . God is merciful . . . his kingdom can change you . . . and I am the Way." And when people missed this—when they started coming to him just to have their pains and problems removed—the Savior often backed away.

No wonder I'd felt so lost. I'd been seeking Jesus to get my problems and paralysis fixed. Yes, Jesus cares about suffering, and he spent most of his time on earth relieving it. But the Gospel of Mark showed me his priorities. The same man who healed blind eyes and withered hands also said, "Gouge out your eye and cut off your hand if it leads you into sin." I got the picture: To me, physical healing had been the big deal. To God, my soul was a *much* bigger deal.

I was *not* an athlete at the core. In an instant, all my physical prowess, my abilities and the medals they earned, meant nothing. I was lost to it. But now . . . who was I?

I started searching for a deeper healing, a Psalm 139 soul-healing: "Search me, O God, and know my heart; test me and see if there is any offensive way in me and lead me in the way everlasting." Right away, I felt ashamed of my root of bitterness and my spirit of complaining. *I don't want to be like that, God,* I prayed. If I was to find myself, I needed to get rid of those sins and more.

I looked to Paul for my example. In Philippians 3:4–8,

he considered that whatever was to his profit was now considered a loss for the sake of Christ. Climbing the social and religious ladder was no longer his focus—he was glad to lose earthly accolades and achievements (his swimming medals, as it were). He called them trash. Paul no longer allowed himself to be defined by his earthly credentials; he considered the whole package a pile of dung compared to knowing Jesus.

And if Paul was to find himself in Christ, it meant "becoming like him in his death" (Phil. 3:10). To do that, he had to die to the sins that Christ died for on his cross. It's what it means to become *like Jesus in his death*. It's all about losing yourself for his sake.

This resonated. And over time, I learned that the core of Christ's plan is to rescue us from sin. Our physical aches and pains and broken relationships are not his ultimate focus—he cares deeply about these things, but they are symptoms of the chief problem in this fallen world. God's goal is not to make us comfortable. He wants to teach us to hate our transgressions as he grows our love for him.

God wants us to hate our sin as much as he does. We see this in Ezekiel 20:26: "I let them become defiled through their gifts—the sacrifice of every firstborn—that I might fill them with horror, so they would know that I am the LORD." Centuries earlier God saw what was coming. Long before the Jews entered Canaan, he knew what they were disposed to do. Why did the Lord permit them to follow their own vices? Especially something so loathsome as child sacrifice, which he hates? He tells us in Ezekiel 20: He permitted them to be drawn away by their desires in order to expose the vileness closeted in their own hearts—all so they would stare at it and be disgusted with themselves. This is a hard point to grasp, but exposing sin is more important to God than relieving human suffering, even unthinkable suffering.[1]

God takes sin far more seriously than we imagine he does. I reread Luke 5 where Jesus healed the paralyzed man lowered by his friends through the roof. This time, I studied the verses I had ignored:

When Jesus saw their faith, he said, "Friend, your sins are forgiven." The Pharisees and the teachers of the law began thinking to themselves, *Who is this fellow who speaks blasphemy? Who can forgive sins but God alone?* Jesus knew what they were thinking and asked, "Why are you thinking these things in your hearts? Which is easier: to say, 'Your sins are forgiven,' or to say, 'Get up and walk?' But I want you to know that the Son of Man has authority on earth to forgive sins." So, he said to the paralyzed man, "I tell you, get up, take your mat and go home." (Luke 5:20–24)

---

1 This principle was first taught to me by Steve Estes, now board member of the Christian Counseling Education Foundation (CCEF) and pastor of Brick Lane Church in Elverson, Pennsylvania.

Jesus could heal the paralyzed man because—and only because—he had authority as the Son of God to forgive sin. It was the point he wanted to make with the Pharisees. For him, healing withered legs would take no more effort than setting stars and moons in motion; for Jesus, it's all merely finger-work (Ps. 8:6). But when it comes to forgiving sin, it was no easy effort for our Savior. Our redemption required gut-spilling blood and a strong arm of salvation (Isa. 63:5).

I collapsed in tears when I began to glimpse how heinous my sin was. Physical healing paled in comparison to the unthinkable abuse my transgressions heaped on my Lord.

So, for the last 50 years in my wheelchair, I've been daily dying to self and rising with Jesus, dying to self and rising with Jesus, dying to self and rising with Jesus.[2] My goal is to mortify my fleshly desires, so I might find myself in Christ. God has been answering my prayer, exposing dark things in my heart, things from which I need to be healed. In fact, remember that root of bitterness, my spirit of complaining? How nothing that anyone did was good enough?

In the first couple years of marriage, my husband, Ken, struggled to keep up with all my disability routines. One night he sat on the edge of our bed, slumped-shouldered, and confessed, "I feel so trapped." Out of nowhere, I spat,

---

[2] Paul Miller in his book *The J Curve: Dying and Rising with Jesus in Every day Life* explains this principle more thoroughly (Wheaton: Crossway, 2019).

"Well, where was your head on our wedding day? Didn't you know it was going to be this hard? You feel trapped? What about *me?!*" Immediately, I felt awful for spouting off and cried, "Oh Ken, I'm so sorry. It's not like me to be that cruel!"

But later the Spirit whispered, "You're wrong, Joni. It's *exactly* like you." God was right. Apart from his Spirit I would say and do all kinds of wicked things. That night I purposed to die *to* pride and selfishness just as Christ died *for* those sins. Years later when I was struggling against cancer, feeling sick and tired, Ken once again became overwhelmed. He confessed, "I feel trapped." But this time I responded, "Oh sweetheart, I don't blame you one bit. I totally understand. I don't fault you for feeling trapped at all. Together, with God's help, we will get through this and be all the better for it."

Every day I am discovering my true self as I partner with the Spirit to experience deeper healing. I consider a sleek, athletic body, and the pride that went with it for me, as rubbish that I may gain Christ and be found in him. "Boasting in the flesh" was—and is—the biggest deterrent to a lively, intimate, and needy dependence on the Lord Jesus. If we want to really pursue Christ, we must learn to hate sin as he does.

God will let you feel much of sin's sting through suffering while you're heading for heaven as a reminder of what you've been saved from, exposing sin for the poison it is.

Thus, one form of evil (your suffering) is turned on its head to defeat another form of evil (your transgressions).

When we let go of sin, we will be found in Christ. We will have reached Jesus's goal, "that [his] joy may be in you and that your joy may be complete" (John 15:11). Jesus is driven to share his joy with you, to have your heart beating in rhythm with his, to have you delight in the indescribable joy of his presence. It's a joy that cascades and overflows your heart, rushing out to others in streams of service and encouragement, then effervescing back to your Savior in an ecstatic fountain of praise. The loss you have suffered will gain you a miracle; you'll be "sorrowful, yet always rejoicing; poor, yet making many rich; having nothing, and yet possessing everything" (2 Cor. 6:10).

Does God miraculously heal? Sure, he does. But in this broken world, it's still the exception, not the rule. A "no" answer to my request for a miraculous physical healing has meant purged sin, a love for the lost, increased compassion, stretched hope, an appetite for grace, an increase of faith, a happy longing for heaven, a desire to serve, a delight in prayer, and a hunger for his Word. Oh, bless the stern schoolmaster that is my wheelchair!

It's all to the praise of deeper healing in Christ.

YOU CAN'T HAVE SOME OF JESUS

BY SAM ALLBERRY

—

"JESUS HAD TO BE EVERYTHING OR ELSE HE'S NOTHING."

Certain things aren't meant to be mixed. Oil and water famously don't get along well. They *can't* be mixed. Other things *shouldn't* be mixed. Take vinegar and bleach. According to an article I recently read ("Everyday Household Products That Can Kill You"—try reading that without becoming terrified of your own kitchen), mixing vinegar and bleach will create toxic chlorine gas. So now I have that to worry about.

Other combinations can also get us in trouble. I work in the historic city of Oxford, England. Recently I walked by one of the rivers, heard a commotion, and discovered a small group of tourists attempting to get into a "punt," a shallow wooden boat maneuvered by someone standing at the back with a long pole to push forward and steer. Because the boats are light and shallow, the mere act of stepping into one is often enough to push it away from the bank, as one of the tourists was discovering to her alarm, for she still had her other foot on the side. A splash quickly resolved the issue. Feet aren't designed to go in two directions at once, at least not for long.

Life is often a matter of trying to find a good balance between its various components. We want to honor those for whom we work and those with whom we live. And our world isn't short of advice, offering everything from "habits of highly effective people" to "rules for life."

But when it comes to our spiritual life there is an even greater danger.

I first heard the gospel of Jesus Christ when I was 17 years old. As a teenager I had gone back and forth about whether I believed in God. At times it didn't seem to make sense, but then I had a nagging feeling that *something* must be out there behind all this. Inasmuch as I knew anything about Jesus, it was that he gave us the Sermon on the Mount to teach us how to live in a moral way, and parables to underline the same points. I knew that he had died on a cross and was assumed to have risen again. But how this fit into anything was not clear.

In the old children's Bible a family member had once given

me, Jesus was portrayed with perfect flowing golden hair and bright teeth. So in my teenage mind he was something of a cross between Gandhi and one of the Bee Gees. Let's face it, a cross between Gandhi and one of the Bee Gees is containable. The "Mahatma Gibb" of my imagination was worthy of being listened to, of following for moral guidance, but not someone who was going to take over.

So it was a shock to discover that the Jesus of the Gospel accounts is quite different. He didn't come merely to offer some ethical advice. He's not someone you can choose your level of involvement with.

He is something else entirely.

ALL OR NOTHING

Consider his first words in Mark's Gospel: "The time is fulfilled, and the kingdom of God is at hand; repent and believe in the gospel" (Mark 1:15).

In the space of half a tweet Jesus shows us this isn't going to be easy. Look at who he says he is. *The time is fulfilled*. Jesus is saying we're in the middle of a saga, rather like when we discovered the first *Star Wars* movie was somehow Episode IV. Time has been waiting for something, Jesus says. The previous centuries have been a story of growing expectation, and *now*—now that *Jesus* is here—it's all being fulfilled. He is what all of history has been waiting for. *The kingdom of God is at hand.* The big-ticket items God had always said he would one day do, he is now going to do . . . because Jesus is here. And this Jesus isn't going to fit into anyone's back pocket. Space, time, and the promises of God all converge on this man.

Now look at what he says about you and me. *Repent.* We're people who, in the light of all that he's just said, need to repent. We're oriented in the wrong direction. We're not lined up with God, so we need to turn back to him. Jesus assumes this is the case for all of us. We might be committed pagans; we might be religious. It doesn't matter. All must come to God.

As I first came to grips with this Jesus, two things were immediately apparent: one was that I didn't know the God who had made me; the other was that this was on me. I *should* know him, and the fact I didn't was my fault. My initial reaction was to realize that the assumptions I'd had about the Christian faith and the person of Jesus needed to be discarded immediately. This wasn't going to be a Jesus I could just slot into my reality without some kind of fight.

I began to realize the very things that made Jesus less easy than I'd thought were what made him so compelling. I couldn't just write him off as demanding when he was so transparently glorious. And I couldn't accuse him of being an egomaniac when he was so stupendously servant-hearted. All of this made one thing obvious: Jesus had to be everything or else he's nothing. There's no in-between.

I was about to turn 18 when this realization hit home. I was sitting at a picnic table and enjoying a summer afternoon. *Christ died for me*, I thought to myself. Those words had now come to mean something. Not just that Jesus died for humanity in some generalized, vague way. But that Jesus had died for *me*. As if I were the only sinner on the planet. He laid down that perfect, provocative, humble life for me. And he'd risen again, as a public vindication and completion of his saving death. If I knew anything, I knew this was someone I could build my future upon. I wanted him in my life.

But here's the thing. Given who he is, you can't have *some* of him. *Some* Jesus is really *no* Jesus at all. He doesn't play that game. He won't be an ingredient in your perfect life. He intends to be no less *than* your perfect life. If we try to combine an "amount" of Jesus with all the other stuff that feels essential to us, we'll end up with something toxic and explosive. It's an unstable compound.

Jesus is humble enough to come to us. But on his terms, not ours. If I was to have him at all, it had to be as a follower, not as co-leader.

So that was that. I gave my life to Christ.

CONTINUE WITH CHRIST

But here's the other thing: Receiving Christ is not the end of the matter of who will lead whom. It turns out the decision I made to follow him that day was one I would need to re-enact every day thereafter—not in the sense of becoming a Christian over and over again, but in the sense of reappropriating what it means to belong to Jesus. That part of me that wanted to combine him with what I already had going on wasn't going to disappear overnight; it tries to reassert itself virtually every day.

The apostle Paul indicated it would be this way: "Therefore, as you received Christ Jesus as Lord, so walk in him, rooted and built up in him and established in the faith, just as you were taught, abounding in thanksgiving" (Col. 2:6–7).

How we start with Christ is how we continue with Christ. The way in is the way on, as they say. We begin by acknowledging the supremacy of Jesus above all things (even if we don't have that sort of language available to us at the time). And we continue each day thereafter in the same way. Jesus comes first.

Jesus makes the same point in the most radical and unmistakable of ways: "If anyone comes to me and does not hate his own father and mother and wife and children and brothers and sisters, yes, and even his own life, he cannot be my disciple. Whoever does not bear his own cross and come after me cannot be my disciple" (Luke 14:26–27).

To be honest, this looks, literally, like hate speech. He is telling us to hate the people closest to us—mom, dad, the rest of the clan, and even our own kids. On its own, this passage makes Jesus look like the sort of preacher many Western countries now routinely ban from entry. But this passage doesn't come on its own.

Elsewhere Jesus makes it clear we have responsibilities to our family members. He rebukes the Pharisees for using their religious devotion as an excuse to neglect providing for their parents:

> Moses said, "Honor your father and your mother"; and, "Whoever reviles father or mother must surely die." But you say, "If a man tells his father or his mother, 'Whatever you would have gained from me is Corban'" (that is, given to God)—"then you no longer permit him to do anything for his father or mother, thus making void the word of God by your tradition that you have handed down." (Mark 7:10–13)

Honoring parents isn't up for negotiation. Whatever the message is in Luke 14, it isn't one that allows us to abandon responsibilities to our families.

So if that's *not* what Jesus is saying, what *is* his point?

Simply this: *He must come first.*

And by come first, he doesn't mean in any contest where things are close. This isn't a photo finish. It's first where the distant second is so distant as to be entirely out of the picture.

Jesus deploys a common Jewish idiom, one we see throughout the Bible. It's a means of emphasizing something by speaking hyperbolically about its opposite. "Jacob I loved, but Esau I hated" is one famous example (Rom. 9:13). Jacob is so loved and chosen that it's as if Esau were hated. Jesus's own prayer contains another example: "Lead us not into temptation but deliver us from evil." It isn't as though God would ever lead us into temptation, for we're told that God tempts no one (James 1:13). No, Jesus's point is to emphasize the deliverance we need from evil.

And so when Jesus calls us to "hate" our parents, family, and our own lives, his point is that we're to love him in such a superlative, unique way that there's no comparison between our love for him and our love for anyone (or anything) else. We love him so much it's *as though we hated* everything else.

Part of being found by Jesus is to realize he's in a league of his own. He's incomparable. We're called to forsake all other allegiances and ties in light of our new life as his disciples. We are his, and not as part of some joint custody arrangement. We are his *utterly*.

This is also reflected in the language about any disciple having to "bear his own cross." Think of how arresting that must have sounded to Jesus's first hearers! They had no familiarity with religious jewelry and crucifixes. Bearing a cross had only one meaning, and that was literal crucifixion. The sight of men carrying crosses to the place they would be killed was common in and around Jerusalem. And yet this is what Jesus uses to describe discipleship. We put him first to the point that we're effectively putting self to death.

DEAL-BREAKER?

So there is a loss to being found. A loss to self. And for many people that can sound like an obvious deal-breaker. We live in a time when we most value authenticity and expressing our individual identity. Western culture, inasmuch as it collectively believes in anything, believes in being true to self. And so these words of Jesus can sound completely unpalatable. Impossible to do, even if we wanted to. Jesus's message is not "You do you!" but "Be made new"; not "Express yourself," but "Deny yourself." This is not always easy to hear.

There were times after my conversion when I wondered if Jesus were worth it. Certain plans and hopes I had for my life weren't coming together through following him. I longed for family, yet I was single and struggling with feelings that made heterosexual marriage unlikely. I wondered if this was worth it; whether I might be better going my own way.

What kept me from doing so was the realization that it would mean going alone. I couldn't bring Jesus down this path with me. I either followed him utterly, submitting this whole area of life and aspiration to him, or I would abandon him utterly, making a decisive break from him and all that I knew him to be. I couldn't have some of his agenda and simply mix it with some of my own.

Think again about what Jesus says to his disciples: "Whoever does not bear his own cross and come after me cannot be my disciple" (Luke 14:27).

In one sense, no one took Jesus up on this warning. None of these original hearers actually followed him all the way to the mount of crucifixion. He hung there alone. And yet that lonely death can utterly transform us. He died alone, because the death he died was a death only he could die as the Son of God—a sin-bearing death on behalf of others (2 Cor. 5:21). When we grasp the fullness of what that death means for us, it cracks open our hearts and reorders everything in our lives. It sows a new selflessness in us, a devotion to what we otherwise might have balked at. Though these original disciples didn't follow Jesus to his cross, once they grasped what he had done for them, they laid down their lives for him and his cause (John 15:13). That is what his death does. It changes us. Being found by Jesus in his death makes us new.

This process is, paradoxically, how we most become our true selves. The process of what Jesus elsewhere calls "denying yourself" (Mark 8:34) doesn't actually mean we become less who we are, but the opposite. We become more who we are, more the person God had in mind in the first place when he originally thought us up. If we cling to ourselves, we will never actually flourish. We'll never be more than a distortion of who God intended us to be; we'll be perpetually lost—to God and to ourselves. But yielding self to Jesus leads to real authenticity. It's a sign of being found.

But the choice is that stark. Jesus first or self first. We embrace him or we don't. What we can't do is have *some* of him. Some combinations don't work, and Jesus won't let us mix him with anything else.

I WOULDN'T TRADE MY SUFFERING

BY VANEETHA RENDALL RISNER

—

"JESUS HEALED THE BLIND MAN. WHAT ABOUT ME?"

I walked up the front steps of our duplex, pretending that everything was okay. I didn't want my mother to know what had just happened; it was too humiliating to talk about. But as we sat at the kitchen table, I kept thinking back to the afternoon and how excited I had been to walk home from school by myself. I was so focused on not falling that I hadn't noticed the group of boys sneaking up behind until they started yelling "Cripple!" and throwing stones at my back. One of them pushed me, and I fell to the ground; the boys immediately scattered. No one bothered to see if I was hurt. I waited for a few minutes to see if anyone would help me, but when no one came, I pulled myself up on a nearby rock and trudged home.

I was 7.

From that moment on, I decided that life wasn't fair. And I was right. Classmates bullied me throughout elementary school—mocking me, imitating my pronounced limp, making me feel like a freak. But I didn't tell my family. What was the point? They couldn't stop the bullying anyway. This was God's fault, if he even existed.

My story begins in India, where I contracted polio as an infant and was left almost completely paralyzed. I spent the first 10 years of life in and out of the hospital, much of it on a crowded ward where I was only allowed to see my parents on weekends. I didn't know which was worse—living in the hospital away from my family or living at home while being tormented at school.

The teasing continued until high school, when I finally felt accepted. People thought I was brave and sweet; they had no idea how angry I was inside. I acted as though I had faith, since I grew up going to church. But God meant nothing to me. I thought everyone was just pretending, that no one really read the Bible or prayed in private. So I was surprised when in high school I went to a meeting of the Fellowship of Christian Athletes (FCA) and heard a classmate talk about her faith in a genuine way. Her father had just died. Yet somehow she felt an inexplicable closeness to God. Jesus was real to her.

For months, her story haunted me. And when a close friend also became a Christian, I knew I needed to rethink my lack of belief. But I still wondered, *If God it is so good, then why am I handicapped?*

MEETING JESUS

I was pondering this thought one night as I lay in bed and finally said aloud, "God, if you are real, please show me." The next morning, I woke up and uncharacteristically opened the Bible. I flipped randomly until I landed on John 9 and began reading. "As he passed by, he saw a man blind from birth. His disciples asked him, 'Rabbi, who sinned, this man or his parents that he was born blind?'"

The passage had my attention. The disciples' question seemed similar to the ones I had heard growing up. Why did I walk that way? What happened to me? What had I done wrong? Their questions were coupled with my own: What had I done to deserve this suffering?

Jesus's answer to the disciples stunned me. "It was not that this man sinned, or his parents, but that the works of God might be displayed in him." Jesus recognized that the blind man's condition wasn't his fault. Rather than condemn him, Jesus honored and dignified him. This blind man's suffering wasn't a punishment; God was going to use his life. The works of God would be displayed in him.

Could God be telling me that my life would display his work as well? It seemed crazy to believe that he would use my pain for something good, but somehow I sensed he would. I knelt at the side of my bed and committed my life to a God I didn't know but who certainly knew me.

I was 16.

DIDN'T GOD OWE ME A PAIN-FREE LIFE?

Now I was excited about the rest of my life. I was sure God would make my life easy and successful. Didn't I deserve it? And at first, I had everything I wanted.

But when I turned 30, my life began to break down. My husband and I went through a serious marriage crisis, and I was afraid we wouldn't make it. After more than a year of intense counseling, when we were finally starting to rebuild trust, our unborn son Paul was diagnosed with a life-threatening heart problem. I wondered to God why I was going through yet another hard thing. What had I done wrong?

Paul had a successful surgery at birth, and the doctors were delighted with his progress. He was doing so well when we took him in for a routine checkup that the substitute doctor took him off his medicine, saying Paul looked great. Though we came home rejoicing, our joy was short-lived. Two days later, Paul woke up in the middle of the night, screamed, and went limp in our arms. We rushed him to the ER, but the

"OUT OF THE UGLINESS OF MY LIFE, GOD BROUGHT BEAUTY."

doctors couldn't revive him. Paul died at just 2 months old.

His death shocked me. I would wake up every night longing to nurse him and hold him. The pain seemed unbearable and inescapable. How could God do this to me? This wasn't the wonderful life I had been counting on. I wanted distance from this God who suddenly felt unpredictable and unsafe.

I pushed God away as long as I could, but finally in desperation I turned back and begged him to meet me. I couldn't do this without him. And he met me once again, just as he had at 16, using the words of John 9. While I didn't know why, I was certain that "[this happened] that the works of God might be displayed in [Paul's death]."

NO OTHER PEACE

Still, how much more could I possibly handle? Next came a post-polio diagnosis, which in the long term would mean complete paralysis and in the short term meant depending on others for basic tasks.

And then my husband of 18 years told me he was leaving for someone else. A few weeks later, he moved to another state. We had worked hard to build love and trust; it seemed impossible that our marriage would crumble. Yet now I was a single parent, with limited physical strength, taking care of two adolescent daughters whose worlds were crashing along with mine. Our once-peaceful home felt like a war zone.

This loss seemed even more unfair than the others, as now there was no one to carry the load with me. How could God love me and let all this happen? Did he even love me? I was exhausted—physically, mentally, and emotionally—as I homeschooled two girls who deeply questioned their faith after our family split.

In my desperation, God showed me his love. I had known God's love and presence for decades, but now I began to turn to him for everything. Although I had a loving community, nothing in my life could really hold me up. No distractions. No hobbies. No relief. The Lord was all I had. And I found he really was enough. I found that sitting with God, reading the Bible, and talking to Jesus made me happier than anything in my life ever had before.

And I realized he's all we ever have, even when it seems like our lives are going well.

We are all lost until Jesus finds us. Through the account of the man born blind, I saw and understood who Jesus is and why he created me. He is the Creator and Redeemer. Through the miracle of his resurrection, Jesus brings life where death has reigned.

Yet Jesus healed the blind man. What about me? I am still

disabled; my body is getting weaker every day. My son died with no "sudden healing." My husband left, and we eventually divorced. To some it may seem that God didn't answer my prayers and that my encounters with Jesus left me unchanged. Yet I know that with each answer of "no," God was doing something deeper in my life. At first, I wanted to run away. But each time I began to wander, I saw how restless and empty I felt without God. There is no lasting peace or contentment apart from Jesus.

Out of the ugliness of my life, God brought beauty. More than anything else he gave me a vibrant, life-giving relationship with himself. And he blessed me in other ways as well. My daughters both came back to the Lord, each with a stronger, more personal faith. A few years ago I married Joel, who tirelessly and lovingly cares for me, even with my increasing disability.

HOW GOD USES SUFFERING

While I would never have chosen suffering, God has used it for my good. Admittedly, my definition of *good* has changed. When I was younger, *good* was whatever made me happy. Whatever was easiest. *Good* was always fun. But now it doesn't depend on pleasant circumstances. *Good* is something with lasting, significant value.

So, what has been good about my suffering? What have my trials done for me?

First, they have refined my character. I am more grateful—I notice and appreciate little things rather than expect them. I'm more compassionate, because I understand how hard it can be even to get out of bed in the middle of loss and pain. I see my weaknesses more clearly, because in suffering my impatience, selfishness, and pride have become apparent. Seeing those weaknesses has been the first step to change, so that I might see God at work in me.

Second, this suffering has taken away my fear of the future. I once thought I could never endure losing a child, losing my marriage, or losing my health and independence. But as each was removed—as my worst nightmares came true—I realized that I could survive. And even more than survive, I could experience joy that does not depend on circumstances, a joy that could never be taken away by anyone or anything.

Third, my suffering has given me a deeper purpose. While my individual struggles are unique, suffering is not exclusive to me. Everyone suffers, and others have endured losses similar to mine. I have sat with fellow sufferers as someone who understands at least some of the emotions and challenges. I can listen with an empathetic ear, offer practical advice, and share the comfort I've received from the Lord. When I have the privilege of helping others, my life feels more significant and meaningful.

These are great benefits, and everyone who has suffered,

Christian or non-Christian, can experience most of them, if willing to accept them. But while I appreciate these gifts, if they were all I gained they probably wouldn't outweigh the pain I've endured. But what completely overshadows my suffering is the fourth gift of suffering: how close it has brought me to Jesus. When my life was easy, God was peripheral to me. My faith was important in theory, but God often felt absent from everyday life. In my losses, I needed God every day. I needed his comfort, his wisdom, his presence. I needed God to give me strength, because I had nothing left.

Every day when I read the Bible, God gave me something to hold on to: a word, a verse, a promise. I had never experienced such intimacy with God before; I didn't even know it existed. I remember sitting at my table one morning, feeling unable to go on when I read Psalm 119:25: "My soul clings to the dust; give me life according to your word!" A strange sense of peace came over me and gave me courage to face the day. I can't begin to put into words how different I felt. God was no longer just a theory, and my faith wasn't only to trust that Jesus would save me from the judgment of sin. My life on the outside may have looked awful, but on the inside it was beautiful.

Finally, my suffering has made me long for heaven. Just being in God's presence will more than compensate for my earthly suffering. In heaven, I will also see in greater clarity how he has used my pain for good, both in my life and also in the lives of others. I will have a new pain-free resurrected body, able to do what I missed out on in this life, like running and painting and making gourmet meals. I will see loved ones and hold my precious son, Paul.

But the greatest joy of heaven won't be any of these things. The greatest joy will be simply being with God. The moments of euphoria with God that I glimpsed on earth will be endless in heaven. Encounters that left me almost floating with joy, blissfully content and at the same time breathless for more of God, will be magnified 10,000 times. No pleasures on earth could ever rival that promised joy.

I am beyond grateful that Christ met me at 16 through John 9 so now I can spend eternity with him. But I'm also grateful for my suffering, because through it God has transformed me and made me love him even more. I echo the words of Joni Eareckson Tada: "I wouldn't trade places with anyone to be this close to Jesus."

CHAPTER 5

THE WAY UP IS DOWN

BY QUINA ARAGON

"I GREW UP BLISSFULLY UNAWARE OF MY INSATIABLE APPETITE FOR STATUS."

What do you want to be when you grow up? We're asked this question often as children. My answer changed from "Firefighter!" (4 years old) to "The world's greatest female soccer player!" (10 years old) to "A successful businesswoman with an office overlooking downtown" (teenager).

Perhaps a helpful follow-up question would have been, "*Why* do you want to be that when you grow up?" I don't think it was a passion to save people from burning buildings, to train and play game after game, or to propel a business into success. It was the idea of appearing great to others, receiving praise, being in charge. Plain and simple: I wanted the glory, the honor, the power.

I grew up blissfully unaware of my insatiable appetite for status. I just wanted to be great and recognized for it. So I excelled in academics. I soared in athletics. I learned how to make people laugh. As one of the few black girls in my private school, I definitely wasn't considered the prettiest. But I figured out how to be popular.

As I stepped into the halls of my huge public high school, however, I was confronted with something I couldn't ignore: I wasn't the fastest, the smartest, or the funniest anymore. Where would I fit in? How would I climb that ladder of status? How would I matter?

Little by little I worked hard at practice and in class. But I was still mostly invisible. So in my sophomore year I dated the popular basketball player, joined clubs, and learned what clothes to wear. One day, a girl in my English class sighed, "I wish I had your life." I did it. I found status again. People wanted to be me. Right?

What she didn't know was that I didn't want to be me. I wanted to be my friends who were even more athletic, more successful, more popular. My inferiority complex haunted me. I wasn't satisfied with status, but I dared not admit it. Could life offer something more?

MY FIRST TASTE OF FREEDOM

I couldn't answer until I met a girl in my junior-year English class who seemed to possess what I didn't: peace, joy, and love. We ended up playing on the same volleyball team that year. As I spent time with her and her family, I witnessed their freedom from the tyranny of trying to seem impressive. They loved freely. I wasn't the successful student-athlete when I visited their house. I was just Quina, beloved friend. I wanted whatever they had.

Soon enough, I learned this freedom could only come through a relationship with Jesus. My friend showed me what the Bible said about me: I was alienated from a perfect God by my sin. I was created to know and love God, giving him the glory and credit in all I do. He alone could satisfy my deepest longings to be known and loved. But I had settled for the praise of people, and I had come up empty.

It finally became clear to me I couldn't even impress God with my attempts at being moral and virtuous. How could I conjure up some sort of holiness to impress the Holy One? I needed him to rescue me from my sin. God let me feel the vacancy in my soul despite my attempts to fill it with worldly acclaim. That emptiness was the alarm that jerked my eyes open to see my desperate need.

My friend pointed me to the God who became a man, who died for me just so I could be his child. What amazing love!

I cast my life—all of my sin and all of my need—on Jesus, and I knew I wanted to live a life of service to him. I took my first sip of satisfying, living water.

UNSPOKEN EXPECTATIONS

Fast forward to my first year after college. I was unemployed. I had no car. I was confused. I had focused much of the past four years on (imperfectly) sharing the good news about Jesus, leading and attending Bible studies, and seeking to serve others while making disciples of Jesus. It's not like I did all of this to the neglect of my studies. I graduated with a near-perfect GPA. But my friends got salaried jobs immediately after graduation. What had I done wrong?

What happens when following Jesus doesn't lead us where we expected to be? How do we cope when following Jesus doesn't seem as rewarding as we thought it would?

Lurking beneath my confusion was an unspoken expectation about following Jesus: Of course he will reward me with a steady income and fulfilling work. When I was granted neither, I became depressed. That haunting inferiority complex reemerged. Why couldn't I be more like my friends who found success after graduating? I wanted companies to recognize and validate my skills with a solid job offer. I wanted my family to applaud my ability to put my diploma to work. If I could make everyone else proud of me, then perhaps I could feel proud about myself.

Beneath my unspoken expectation was a deep desire to feel important and accomplished. I knew I hadn't been satisfied with status in the past, but I longed for it again anyway. Something in me wanted to ensure I could secure special status in Jesus's kingdom. How else would my life count?

ASKING THE WRONG QUESTIONS

I wasn't much different from the mother of James and John when she asked Jesus to give her sons distinct rank in his kingdom: "Say that these two sons of mine are to sit, one at your right hand and one at your left, in your kingdom" (Matt. 20:21).

She herself was a faithful follower of Jesus who ministered to his needs on the way to Jerusalem (Matt. 27:55–56). Perhaps she remembered how Bathsheba secured her son Solomon's throne by appealing to King David (1 Kings 1:15–21). She may have even been Jesus's aunt.[3] Her sons, along with Peter, were Jesus's closest friends.[4] Jesus had just promised them thrones in the kingdom (Matt. 19:28). Peter had already been sharply rebuked by Jesus in front

---

[3] Cf. Mark 15:40; 16:1; John 19:25

[4] See Matt. 4:18–22; 10:2; 17:1; 26:37; Mark 5:37; 13:3.

of the other disciples (Matt. 16:21–23). So that had to leave James and John as Jesus's favorites, destined to sit on either side of the King of kings . . . right?

Like me, she and her sons seemed to have missed Jesus's persistent teaching about the nature of his kingdom. This paradoxical kingdom would be inherited by the poor in spirit, the mourning, and the meek (Matt. 5:2–12). The greatest would be the smallest (Matt. 18:1–4), and the first would be the last (Matt. 19:28–30). Jesus would rule an upside-down kingdom, flipping human expectations on their head.

"So Jesus answered, 'You do not know what you are asking. Are you able to drink the cup that I am to drink?' James and John answered, 'We are able.'" (Matt. 20:22). They knew from the Scriptures that the cup Jesus referred to was a cup of suffering (Isa. 51:21; Lam. 4:21). Jesus had made it clear they must all suffer for his name's sake (Matt. 10:16–25, 38; 16:24). Sincere as they may have been, they were still naive about how suffering would tempt them to abandon Jesus.

Jesus admitted that James and John would indeed drink Jesus's cup of suffering (Acts 12:2). But he didn't want them to focus on how rewards for serving Jesus will be doled out in the kingdom. "To sit at my right hand and at my left is not mine to grant," he told them, "but it is for those for whom it has been prepared by my Father" (Matt. 20:23).

They were concerned about how they would be honored in comparison to the others. Jesus wanted them to think about something totally different (cf. Matt. 19:27–20:16).[5] In other words, they were asking the wrong question.

When the other 10 disciples found out that James and John made this request, they were livid (Matt. 20:24). Apparently, they'd all managed to only hear what they wanted to hear about the Christ: "The Son of Man will sit on his glorious throne, and you who have followed me will also sit on twelve thrones" (Matt. 19:28). Their desire for renown was fueled by persistent ignorance regarding the true nature of Jesus's kingdom, mission, and identity.

I was taught that following Jesus meant suffering in various ways. I knew intellectually that trusting him didn't keep me from trials. When I first began growing in my faith, I often said rather boldly, like James and John: "I will suffer for you, Jesus! I'll die for you!" Yet here I was with a dull diploma and deep debt, doubting the goodness of God. I kept wondering, *What did I do wrong? Why isn't God blessing me like he's blessing my friends?* I was asking the wrong questions.

---

5 Jesus had addressed the importance of leaving the distribution of rewards to God prior to this encounter when he answered Peter's question, "What then will we have?" (Matt. 19:27). Jesus would not forget the sacrifices of his disciples. They would be rewarded. But *how* they would be rewarded in relation to other followers shouldn't be their concern. Jesus then illustrated his paradoxical phrase, "Many who are first will be last, and the last first" (Matt. 19:30), with a parable in Matthew 20:1–16. Rewards for serving God are to be expected (see also John 12:26), but their distribution is up to the Master who knows and does what is best.

What I truly needed to ask was this: Who is this Jesus I said I'd follow, and what does it really mean to follow him?

TRUE GREATNESS

And that's what Jesus intended to teach me, as he had previously taught his disciples. Left unchecked, their jockeying for position would leave them no different than the religious leaders Jesus so searingly critiqued (Matt. 23:1–36). Their thirst for power and pomp would make them no better than their Roman oppressors. Their pride would lie to the world about the character of the Christ. Their rivalry would wreck the mission.

So Jesus, as usual, turned their understanding of greatness upside down: "You know that the rulers of the Gentiles lord it over them, and their great ones exercise authority over them. It shall not be so among you. But whoever would be great among you must be your servant, and whoever would be first among you must be your slave" (Matt. 20:25–26). The path to greatness and glory is a path of humble service and suffering.

Jesus didn't condemn ambition altogether. He wanted his disciples to pursue greatness. But he clarified what true greatness is and how it's achieved. True greatness is a lifestyle of serving others over yourself. This is what it means to follow Jesus.

WHO IS THIS SON OF MAN?

This call to suffer and serve is hard to hear, and even harder to apply. But Jesus trod the path of pain first. He told his disciples they must focus on sacrificial service to others, not just because he said so, but because he would do so. They must serve "even as the Son of Man came not to be served but to serve, and to give his life as a ransom for many" (Matt. 20:28). When Jesus tells his disciples, "Follow me," he goes first.

Jesus would embody his own teaching when he got to Jerusalem. He had already revealed to his disciples that he must go to Jerusalem to suffer, be killed, and be raised on the third day. But a suffering Christ wasn't the King they were expecting.

Perhaps this is why Jesus so often called himself the "Son of Man." With this title, Jesus could clarify his identity and mission (Dan. 7:13–14). Yes, the Son of Man was the promised King, but this meant that he must first become God's suffering servant, as the prophet Isaiah foretold (Isa. 53).

The glory and honor of the Messiah would be most fully displayed after he accomplished the humiliating, excruciating task of paying for sins with his own life. He would be humbled before he would be exalted (Phil. 2:5–11). The cross would come before the crown, even—especially—for the Christ.

That the Son of Man must first "be lifted up" via crucifixion caused many to reject Jesus (John 12:32). After all, what kind of authority can someone claim as he hangs naked on a bloody Roman cross? In their unbelief the crowds asked, "We have heard from the Law that the Christ remains forever. How can you say that the Son of Man must be lifted up? Who is this Son of Man?" (John 12:34).

Jesus told his disciples who this Son of Man is: the One who came "to give his life as a ransom" (Matt. 20:28). Although he called James and John to drink a cup of suffering, Jesus's cup was unique. In his was the foaming wrath of God for the sins of his people—past, present, and future.[6] On the cross, Jesus suffered under the full weight of God's righteous anger for sin. He drained this cup down to the dregs. In doing so, he gave his life as a ransom, or payment, to free us from bondage to sin and death.[7]

His resurrection on the third day proved that Jesus truly is "the Christ, the Son of the living God" (Matt. 16:16) who paid our sin debt in full. All who put their trust in this Son of Man find freedom that no amount of money, political power, or fame can buy.

---

6 See Ps. 75:8; Matt. 26:36–46; 47:45–46; John 18:11; Rev. 14:10; 16:19.

7 See Ps. 49:7–9; 15; John 19:30; Col. 2:13–15; 1 Tim. 2:5–6; 1 Pet. 1:18–19.

"GOD CREATED US WITH AN INSATIABLE APPETITE FOR GREATNESS THAT CAN ONLY BE FULFILLED IN HIM."

WAY UP

Jesus's disciples eventually grasped the paradoxical character of his kingdom. Little by little, I think I'm getting there too. After about six months of post-college unemployment, I landed an administrative job at a hospital. This wasn't my dream job by any stretch of the imagination. I've never had any burning desire to work on schedules and spreadsheets in a small room tucked behind the ER. But as I worked an unglamorous job behind the scenes for three years, Jesus continued to teach me that true satisfaction will never come from recognition or the praise of people. He showed me there's no station in life so small that God can't use it for his glory if my aim is to serve him as I serve others.

I now see that while I was asking "What did I do wrong?" and "Why is this happening?" Jesus was graciously calling me into that same huddle with his disciples to answer far greater questions: "Who is this Son of Man?" and "What does it mean to be great?"

The mother of James and John asked for her sons to be privileged. The other disciples wanted the same. If we're honest, we want it too. We're wired with ambition; we want our lives to count; we want to be great in some way. Behind these cravings for significance is a longing to be intimately, deeply, eternally known. God created us with an insatiable appetite for greatness that can only be fulfilled in him.

Are you struggling with where the Lord has you today? Jesus welcomes your cries, your confusion, your questions, and your requests. He is fully aware that we often call out to him with misguided questions and concerns, as did the mother of James and John. Yet he still calls us to know him through prayer, his Word, and his people. He punctures our pride, reminds us that his ultimate sacrifice bought our forgiveness, and sets us back on the path of humble service for his glory.

If we want the work of our hands to endure, if we want the labor of our lives to be praised, if we want the glory that comes from God, then we must follow our Savior's example of sacrificial service. He calls his followers to pursue faithfulness over fame, devotion over dominance, sacrifice over status. The humble will be exalted. The way up is down.

CHAPTER 6

WHO IS THE NEIGHBOR?

BY CHRISTOPHER YUAN

"HOW WERE MY PARENTS ABLE TO LOVE A COMPLETE STRANGER— EVEN ONE LIVING IN SIN?"

I wish I could forget the smell of urine from that spring day in 1996. A few years would pass before I received the call of salvation. I was back in my hometown of Chicago and, for the first time, at the old Cook County Hospital. The run-down building was more like a haunted house than a hope-filled place of healing.[8]

My good friend Jordan had fallen sick. He was a well-known gay entertainer, but few knew he was HIV-positive. After several performances in the Windy City, Jordan came down with pneumonia—a life-threatening situation for someone with a compromised immune system. So he landed at Cook

---

8 Adapted from Christopher Yuan, *Holy Sexuality and the Gospel: Sex, Desire, and Relationships Shaped by God's Grand Story* (Colorado Springs: Multnomah, 2018).

County—not a place for the rich and famous, but a catch-all medical institution for people in need.

Taking a few days off from dental school, I drove up from Louisville to see him. I was told Jordan was quarantined in the intensive care unit. After putting on a mask, gown, and gloves, I saw him lying in the bed. What shocked me most wasn't that my friend—normally young and strong—looked tired and emaciated. It's that he was completely alone.

There was no one with him. None of his thousands of fans. None of his many friends from the parties. None of the other entertainers in the industry. Not even his own family. I couldn't help but think, *Will my end as a gay man be like this? All alone?*

I stayed the night with Jordan in the cold, dreary hospital room. Before he awoke, I was compelled to call home for some outlandish reason. I knew where my parents stood when it came to sexuality, but I just wanted to hear a familiar voice. Dad and Mom were fairly new Christians; as a matter of fact, a catalyst to their conversion was my coming-out declaration in 1993. At first, they rejected me; but after coming to Christ, they had a change of heart and *annoyingly* pursued me.

So when I called from Cook County Hospital, my mother was so excited I was in Chicago; she and Dad would come see us right away. I was a bit shocked; I never expected she would be so eager to meet any of my gay friends. Before long, my parents were outside the intensive care unit getting gowned up. I was so worried they might say something that would offend Jordan, especially in his vulnerable state.

But my anxiety vanished when my mom made eye contact with Jordan. Her eyes, just peeping over the surgical mask, were full of compassion and love. She and Dad gave me a big hug; then they crossed the room to Jordan's bed, leaned over, and gave him a big hug as well. We sat for more than half an hour chatting and laughing. My parents brought up no sensitive topics. We just talked like old friends.

SURPRISING QUESTION

How were my parents able to love a complete stranger— *even one living in sin*? One of Jesus's well-known parables is about loving strangers. It's the story of the good Samaritan—a quintessential example of exhibiting compassion to someone in need. The key detail lies in Jesus's final question to the lawyer.

This question alters the crux of this narrative that many think they know so well. As a matter of fact, Jesus's parables aren't meant to make us comfortable or feel good. They're meant to provoke us out of our comfort zone to consider, *What still needs to change in my life?*

Before we get to the question Jesus asks at the end of the parable, look at the question posed to Jesus before it. In Luke 10:25, an expert in Mosaic law tries to test Jesus by asking, "What shall I do to inherit eternal life?" Instead, Jesus tests the tester: "What is written in the Law? How do you read it?" Having probably heard Jesus before, the lawyer responds by mentioning the two greatest commandments: Love God and love your neighbor.

Before we know it, though, the lawyer pounces with this question: "Who is my neighbor?" To justify his lack of compassion, the lawyer really wants to know who is *not* his neighbor. Here is Jesus's response:

> A man was going down from Jerusalem to Jericho, and he fell among robbers, who stripped him and beat him and departed, leaving him half dead. Now by chance a priest was going down that road, and when he saw him he passed by on the other side. So likewise a Levite, when he came to the place and saw him, passed by on the other side. But a Samaritan, as he journeyed, came to where he was, and when he saw him, he had compassion. He went to him and bound up his wounds, pouring on oil and wine. Then he set him on his own animal and brought him to an inn and took care of him. And the next day he took out two denarii and gave them to the innkeeper, saying, "Take care of him, and whatever more you spend, I will repay you when I come back." (Luke 10:30–35)

First, let's recall what prompted this parable: the lawyer's question, "Who is my neighbor?" From the story, the answer seems simple. The good Samaritan saw the traveler who fell among the robbers as his neighbor. It seems obvious, then, that anyone in need is our neighbor. But there is a key detail often missed in Jesus's final question. If he meant the beat-up traveler to be the neighbor, then we'd expect Jesus to ask, "Which of these three, do you think, treated the man who fell among the robbers as his neighbor?"

This is not the question Jesus asks. Instead, he asks: "Which of these three, do you think, proved to be a neighbor to the man who fell among the robbers?"

Observe the difference. Jesus is a master storyteller, and as he often does, he turns the scenario on its head with a provocative twist. In a surprising reversal of roles, the neighbor isn't the traveler who fell among the robbers; the neighbor is the Samaritan.

The parable has a profound thrust, particularly in light of the fact that Jews regarded Samaritans among the least respected people—eating with them was equivalent to eating pork.[9] Yet the parable's significance is much more than simply teaching us to transcend our human-made boundaries of race or social status to love a complete stranger.

---

[9] Darrell L. Bock, *Luke 9:51–24:53*, Baker Exegetical Commentary on the New Testament 3B (Grand Rapids: Baker Academic, 1996), 1031.

KEY TO THE STORY

Jesus knew it was next to impossible for this Jewish lawyer to go against his human nature to love the unlovable Samaritan unless something radical happened in his life. The key is found within the story, particularly the point of view from which it's told—not from the perspective of the good Samaritan but from the perspective of the dying traveler.[10]

The only way for the Jewish lawyer to love a despised Samaritan as his neighbor was to relive this parable from that traveler's point of view. More than likely, the man who fell among the robbers was Jewish himself and therefore hated Samaritans. One day on his way to Jericho, he's jumped by a gang of thugs and knocked unconscious. The last thing he remembers is his nose being crushed by punches and the pain of his ribs cracking from kicks to the gut.

This is it . . . I'm going to die.

Now imagine him waking up confused, lying in a warm bed. A stranger who says he's an innkeeper quickly brings him food and drink, then tends to his wounds. Still in excruciating pain, the man is shocked to be alive. Assuming this innkeeper saved his life, the traveler begins

---

10 Bock, *Luke 9:51–24:53*, 1021.

to thank him. But what comes out of the innkeeper's mouth changes his life forever.

The innkeeper tells him a Samaritan stopped, had compassion, bound the man's wounds, and brought him to this inn. This Samaritan even promised to pay the full amount necessary for the traveler to be cared for until he is fully healed.

Let that sink in. You tell me: Would the man who fell among the robbers be changed when he heard this news? Would this traveler—a Samaritan-despising Jew—now have a totally different perspective toward Samaritans, or any other stranger for that matter?

With this in mind, let's answer the question again: *Who is my neighbor?* I bet if the lawyer really put himself in the shoes of the traveler, he'd have a completely different perspective on life. Jesus isn't exhorting us simply to love a complete stranger in need; he commands us to love people we perceive to be despised, undeserving, and foreign.

Jesus subtly and creatively communicates that the only way we can love our neighbor—the only way a Jew can love a despised Samaritan or a Christian can love a complete stranger—is to put ourselves in the shoes of the man who fell among the robbers. So let's do just that.

I was going down from Jerusalem to Jericho, and *I* fell

among robbers, who stripped *me* and beat *me* and departed, leaving *me* half dead. Now by chance a priest was going down that road, and when he saw *me* he passed by on the other side. So likewise a Levite, when he came to the place and saw *me*, passed by on the other side. But a Samaritan, as he journeyed, came to where *I* was, and when he saw *me*, he had compassion. He went to *me* and bound up *my* wounds, pouring on oil and wine. Then he set *me* on his own animal and brought *me* to an inn and took care of *me*. And the next day he took out two denarii and gave them to the innkeeper, saying, "Take care of *this individual*, and whatever more you spend, I will repay you when I come back."

If we're honest, what happened to this traveler isn't much different from what has happened to each and every one of us in God's redemptive story. Sin has robbed us, beaten us, and left us dead at the side of the road. Everyone we might expect to help has passed us by. But one person stopped and had compassion.

His name is Jesus.

Jesus even paid the ultimate price of his own life so we would be healed. Only when we find solidarity with the traveler who fell among the robbers, realizing Jesus is the good Samaritan showing compassion, are we truly able to love our neighbor as ourselves.

The main takeaway of this parable isn't to love your neighbor by trying hard to be like the good Samaritan. Rather, love your neighbor by realizing you are the traveler, and Jesus—the good Samaritan—has loved you first.

DARKNESS TO LIGHT

When I came out to my parents in 1993, the timing couldn't have been worse. My parents had already begun the paperwork for a divorce after 28 years of marriage. And for my mom, my announcement was the straw that broke the camel's back. She resolved to do the unthinkable; she was going to end her life.

For some reason, she felt the need to see a minister, who gave her a pamphlet on homosexuality that shared the gospel message. She was struck by the realization that she was a sinner herself, yet God still loved her. Thus God opened the eyes of her heart, and she recognized that just as he loved her, she could love me in spite of living as a gay man.

That day my mother received the gift of faith, which enabled her to love me as God loved her. Although many years of anguish and turmoil brought her to desperation, she remained steadfast in pursuing Christ and being saturated in God's Word. She fasted every Monday for seven years and even fasted 39 days on my behalf. Things progressively got worse before they got better.

My mother prayed that God would do whatever it took to bring me to full surrender, and the answer was my imprisonment for drug dealing. But God used prison to bring me to my knees, and because of my parents' persistent witness over many years, I began to consider and receive the gospel truths found in Scripture. And while I was locked up, God brought me from unbelief to belief, death to life, darkness to light.

The narrative is often told of Christian parents rejecting their gay children and being unloving, while unbelieving parents really love and support their gay sons and daughters. I experienced the exact opposite. Before my mother came to Christ, she rejected me; only *after* her conversion did she love her gay son and show compassion to a complete stranger.

When my parents showed compassion to Jordan, a total stranger, they didn't do it by mustering up goodness from the depths of their own hearts. They did it because they realized they're sinners too, just as broken as the man who fell among robbers. They loved Jordan and me because Jesus loved them first. Their love overflowed from Christ's abundant love for them.

Understanding the parable in this way, we realize that loving our neighbor begins not by being like the good Samaritan but by being the man who fell among the robbers. In essence, to save others we need to be saved first! Love doesn't come from the goodness within our own hearts. Love reflects the One who loved us first.

CHAPTER 7

THE RESTING PLACE

—

BY CHRIS CASTALDO

"I RECOGNIZED GOD AS MORE THAN THE PLASTER STATUE NEAR THE ALTAR, BUT ALL THE PLASTER MADE IT DIFFICULT TO KNOW WHAT HE WAS LIKE."

I t was Karl Marx who said that in all human history, no country has sustained such unrelenting slavery, conquest, and foreign oppression as Sicily. Granting the possibility of some hyperbole, it's a matter of historical fact that Sicily has been invaded, ravaged, sacked, and humiliated in virtually every century.

Consider Giovanna, a resident of Castelvetrano in the year 1902. She sits on her doorstep under the blazing sun, clothed in rags, her face yellowed by malaria. Her brown eyes are melancholy, and her swollen stomach is drawn tight like a drum. Inside the home is Giovanna's older sister, Teresa, who lies on the floor beneath a torn blanket, undernourished, teeth chattering from fever. An inescapable pessimism defines their existence, a product of starvation's suffocating stranglehold.

Frustrated by their unending *miseria* (poverty), enterprising peasants heard about *La Merica* and began to look for a long-term solution beyond the Sicilian shore. Men usually went first. Mothers hung on to trains departing from the station—a gesture of their affection and recognition that such goodbyes were likely final. Hunger, seasickness, and sorrow defined each transatlantic journey. Immigrants arriving in New York found dark, overcrowded tenements, rife with tuberculosis and typhoid. Food was scarce. Daily sustenance typically consisted of the *acqua sale*—stale bread moistened in boiling water with a bit of salt and olive oil for flavor.

New York, the cradle of opportunity, offered to liberate immigrants from the shackles of poverty, but not without its own path of *miseria*. A great swirl of hope and adversity, gold and dirt, pathos and pity—for most people it was a menial and demoralizing grind. As a young man, my grandfather Francesco learned the chief means by which one could escape: hard work and personal charisma. He and his brother Vito started a restaurant and soon found customers with an appetite for his recipe.

My grandfather's drive for success was motivated by a desire deeper than survival. It reached back to his nascent years, even to Castelvetrano, from which his family had come. Nearly two decades had passed since his parents immigrated, but the shards of shame remained embedded in their psyche, a mode of thinking and self-understanding reinforced in countless ways. Success in *La Merica* was thus a way of taking revenge on the past, a way for my grandfather to demonstrate his worth. It therefore wasn't comfort that fueled his enterprising spirit, so much as the opportunity to climb from the pits of humiliation and realize his potential in the sight of family, friends, the world, and the angels.

A fascinating wonder of life is the way patterns often recapitulate through the generations. My dad, like my grandfather, became an entrepreneur. Applying the recipe of hard work and personal charisma, he sold printing by day and ran the press at night. For the first year of my life, he would come home on weekends, bounce me on his knee, and get back to work. In this way, he built a successful business. Is it any wonder that *Rocky* would become our favorite movie? "Yo Adrian, I just want to prove I'm not another bum from the neighborhood."

I think of my childhood as an opera. My mother talked in arias, and Puccini's *Nessun Dorma* ("None shall sleep") was the melodic impulse of our experience. Any laxity or lack of ambition hastened apocalypse—none shall sleep until the world is conquered. And why expend yourself to this extent? The climactic moment of Puccini's aria provides the answer: "Vincerò" ("I will win"). It was simply the cost of dissolving our shame and winning the day.

IN PURSUIT OF GOD

Like most other Italians in New York, I was raised Roman Catholic. Men in collars, women in habits, and the bishop with his stylized staff composed our home team. Monsignor Tom, our parish priest, faithfully shepherded our family. And then there was Deacon Sal, the size of a door, receding hairline and a giant meatball face. He had long ago lost his tenderness, his eyes once aflame but now extinguished. Religion, for Sal, appeared to be more duty than delight. When explaining to our youth group the requirements of heaven, he pointed to religious giants such as Francis Xavier, Thomas More, and Padre Pio—saints and martyrs who secured God's favor through tireless effort.

I recognized God as more than the plaster statue near the altar, but all the plaster made it difficult to know what he was like. Under an image of Jesus's Sacred Heart, I lit candles at the brass table terraced with rows of red glowing glasses. In that ambient light, the searching eyes of Christ seized my attention, and a question crossed my mind. The voice, however, was Sal's: "Who do you think you're fooling?" The expressionless portrait of Christ (which some describe as the "disapproving Jesus") looked down into my soul. Feeling vulnerable, I searched for mercy in the contours of Jesus's face, a face that seemed to want something I didn't have.

Days became months, and months became years.[11] At age 19, a mysterious illness landed me in the hospital. Breathing became difficult as my lungs gradually filled with fluid. A rotation of doctors shuffled through my room asking diagnostic questions. After several hours of bewildered expressions, I was moved to a quarantine area where visitors were required to wear medical face masks. The panic in everyone's eyes was noticeable. Feeling anxious, I gazed through my second-story window at a branch that had lost most of its leaves to the winter wind. My mind went to the picture of Jesus's Sacred Heart.

Weeks in the hospital led me to question life's meaning. *Why was I alive? Is there really a God, and if so, what does it take to earn his favor?* With each day, questions grew and eventually settled into a resolution to find answers. By the time the young nurse rolled my wheelchair through the exit doors of the hospital, the spiritual quest was underway.

The first step of my quest was to pursue transcendental meditation under the Maharishi Mahesh Yogi. After a few months of making unusual noises in a lotus position, I understood why the Beatles became disenchanted with Mr. Yogi's method. The apex of my spiritual journey was a "Fire Walk." It was at New York's Jacob Javits Center,

---

11 Taken from *Holy Ground* by Chris Castaldo. Copyright © 2009 by Christopher A. Castaldo. Used by permission of Zondervan. www.zondervan.com

where more than a thousand people waited to hear motivational speaker Tony Robbins. After three hours of his encouraging affirmations, neuro-linguistic programming, and some New Age meditation, our massive herd shuffled outside to the parking lot, where we encountered long stretches of burning coals and embers. According to Robbins, the experience was designed to be a "metaphor" for overcoming our fears and improving life. Never before had a metaphor looked so harmful.

When the lady ahead of me proceeded to walk across the 12-foot path of fire, I inhaled deeply. Tony Robbins's wife (who happened to be facilitating my line) put her hand on my shoulder and said, "You can do this!" I noticed that she was wearing shoes and was at least 20 inches from the nearest coal; nevertheless, I stepped forward and moved as quickly as my trembling legs could carry me. I don't know how it worked; all I can say is that I walked across the fire without getting burned. Despite the thrill, however, the longing of my heart persisted.

ROAD TO CALVARY

My journey down the road to Calvary started one morning. Upon reaching my office in Manhattan, the phone rang. It was my grandfather. In a serious tone, he delivered a brief message: "It's your dad; come home." Somehow, I knew not to ask questions. It turned out to be a severe heart attack, and the waterline of anxiety quickly rose above my head.

After days of sitting beside Dad's hospital bed, I left my job at New York Telephone to manage the family business—a mid-size printing company with a dozen employees. With a deepening level of stress, Mom's emotions crashed, and I started having panic attacks. But into this valley appeared a new employee named Jan, who I soon learned was a Christian.

One day, as I ended another call with the cardiologist's office, I noticed a handwritten index card on my desk:

> Come to me, all who labor and are heavy laden, and I will give you rest. Take my yoke upon you, and learn from me, for I am gentle and lowly in heart, and you will find rest for your souls. For my yoke is easy, and my burden is light. (Matt. 11:28–30)

It was from Jan. Each day she selected a Bible verse and left it for me. I normally would have dismissed her notes as religious propaganda from a flaky employee. But now, after weeks of despair, I was attentive and collected them in my desk. I returned to this passage, and finally asked Jan about it: "How does one experience the rest of God?" Jan opened her Bible and began to explain. "Notice, Chris, what precedes Jesus's statement concerning rest. In these verses, Christ confronts the arrogance of the scribes and Pharisees. Proud of themselves and their tradition, they looked down from Moses's seat, particularly upon an upstart rabbi such as Jesus:

> For John [the Baptist] came neither eating nor drinking, and [these religious leaders] say, "He has a demon." The Son of Man came eating and drinking, and they say, "Look at him! A glutton and a drunkard, a friend of tax collectors and sinners!" (Matt. 11:18–19)

Can you hear them? *Look at that rabbi from Nazareth. Fraternizing with prostitutes and drunkards.*

This observation was interesting coming from Jan. She had shared her story with me once before, how she had been a prostitute in earlier years before undergoing a radical conversion during the 1970s charismatic renewal movement. "Isn't this how the world speaks to us?" Jan continued. "It's all about shame. And isn't this the way we speak to ourselves? The relentless whisper of our conscience bears witness to innumerable ways we are unworthy."

"But look at Jesus," she exclaimed. "He doesn't play the Pharisees' game. Instead, he thanks God for revealing the wonder of redemptive grace to children. Why children? Because unlike us, they are not taking revenge on their past. More innocent and trusting, they accept love without having to earn it." At that precise moment, someone entered my office. Our conversation ended, but not before Jan invited me to visit her church on Wednesday night. Naturally disposed to decline, I listened as the word proceeded from my mouth in response to her invitation. I, more than anyone else, was surprised by what I heard: "Yes."

CHRIST, OUR VICTORY

The parking lot of Faith Church was packed. In amazement, I looked around. *It's a Wednesday night; who are these people?* With a mixture of humiliation and curiosity I entered the building and sat in the rear pew of their "worship center." Devoid of any wood carvings, arched windows, or stained glass, it was simply a large room with a stage. Worse than austere, it was ugly. Never had I felt more out of place in church—like a pork chop in a synagogue.

Occasionally, I looked through my peripheral vision at Jan. Her eyes remained closed as she sang. Oh, and did we sing! After 40 minutes of choruses that seemed familiar to everyone but me, the senior pastor finally entered the pulpit. With a style combining Al Pacino and a young Billy Graham, he quoted several verses, including Matthew 11:28: "Come to me, all who labor and are heavy laden, and I will give you rest."

The preacher continued, explaining why we can have the audacity to approach Jesus—because he is "gentle and lowly in heart."

The profound humility of Christ is displayed in the fact that before instructing us to take his yoke, he took it up for us—that rough hewn beam of wood, laid upon his shoulders and neck. We call it the "old rugged cross," that instrument of Roman torture. On it, Jesus died for our guilt and shame.

It seemed that he was speaking directly to me as he expressed the following:

In what are you resting? What will be there for you the second after you take your final breath and depart in death? Hear the good news! Jesus not only died, but rose from the dead, reigns in eternal glory, and at this moment is calling you to himself.

I don't know how to properly describe what came next. Anticipation surged through my veins, and my mind swirled with questions. Then, suddenly, the eyes of my soul opened. They immediately blinked, again, and again, as though woken from sleep by a flash of light. The object of my vision appeared so new and bright that my initial response was to retreat.

As my inner eyes tried to adjust, I sensed an imposing presence. I didn't see the angelic host or hear them singing. Instead, I felt divine mercy drawing close. After a moment, this mercy, now accompanied by grace, reached out to grasp my guilt and shame—previously reasons for despair—and it brought to mind three simple words: "It is finished." At once, the shackles of condemnation lost their grip, and the shards of shame began to dissolve. Similar to converts like Augustine, Pascal, Luther, Newton, and a host of others throughout history, I encountered God in such a profound way that my life was permanently changed.

It wasn't long after my conversion that Grandpa died. By this time, Dad's health had improved, and within months he came to faith in Christ, as did my mother and sister. Together, we drove to the funeral parlor with heavy hearts. Art, poetry, music—all the progenitors of human awareness and inspiration can't adequately capture the intense emotion of a loved one's funeral. So it was.

Perhaps the most poignant moment occurred when my five cousins and I carried Grandpa's casket into the church. Six Italian boys, whom he once carried to our little sleeping bags after a long night of dancing the *tarantella*, now carefully bore his body toward its final resting place. Monsignor Tom spread the pall over the casket, the white cloth symbolizing the righteousness of Christ in which believers are clothed on account of the resurrection. The embroidered cross in the center of the fabric captured my attention. It occurred to me, no longer are we defined by the great swirl of *miseria*. No longer condemned to taking revenge on the past. Christ is risen. Our guilt and shame have been covered. The great victory has been won. *Vincerò*.

CHAPTER 8

A MILLION BUTTERFLIES ON THE WAY HOME

BY AIXA DE LÓPEZ

"IT'S THE MOST MISERABLE LIVING, SWEARING YOU LIVE FOR JESUS WHILE BEING TOTALLY OBLIVIOUS TO WHO HE REALLY IS."

I hear her laughter downstairs, and my stomach begins to churn. She's supposed to be coloring planets for the science project, but she's way too enthralled by something else. I start to feel mean butterflies in my stomach, a kind of species opposite to those you get when you're in love. When she laughs, I worry. Because she laughs at things she should be sad about. She delights in stuff that probably will hurt her and demean someone else. She still can't quite tell the difference between true joy and evil entertainment. I hear her laughing, and I start to wonder what I'll find when I finally work up the strength to once again march downstairs.

She's about to turn 13 but came to us at 9, so we are still

in the thick of an ongoing struggle to create new pathways in her brain that lead her in a different direction—one of wisdom, thoughtfulness, and obedience. But most of all, we are in a fierce battle for her heart. Her great need is to learn to trust and be guided. She has yet to be convinced she needs us. Indeed, she has begun to experience the clash of her old joys and her new life with us.

Adoption is a brutally honest teacher. And, oh, we are surely learning! Not so much about competent caregiving, but about how little we know our own darkness and mostly about the amazing journey God undertook in order to bring us to his family. He knew how much evil is in our stubborn, self-serving hearts—and how much it was going to cost him personally. That unparalleled love leaves me speechless on a regular basis now.

This little girl is my daughter. And I am God's. Her laughter makes my stomach hurt, and my evil joys make God's heart break. I had a vague idea of how much parenting ex-orphans would hurt. But God? He was absolutely certain of what it would entail. He always knew the whole story. He counted the cost and still chose to make the appointment, put on his coat, and grab his keys. I have learned to look at my daughter and see my reflection, because I too was born with an orphan heart. That's our default mode even if, like me, you were blessed with loving biological parents who sought to nourish you. We run from God because we believe the lie that sin programmed us to believe: *I can take care of myself, and I'll be happier if I run away from him.*

FAKE FAMILY PORTRAIT

Don't be fooled by what people in my surroundings thought of me or what my family portrait showed. I was all grown up on the outside and married to a pastor. And not just a pastor but the founding pastor's son, which means all the ladies who saw him growing up prayed for whomever his wife was going to be. At 6 years old I was probably learning a joke with a dirty word in it while he was winning another Bible quiz at vacation Bible school. As a grown mother of two babies and participating in the women's meetings, I was still the proud owner of an orphan heart that delighted in the wrong things and kept walking in the wrong direction.

No, I didn't commit adultery or rob a bank or any other blockbuster sin. But make no mistake: I was lost. I'd had my run as a typically wild teen who came back ashamed to recommit her life at a church youth camp. I could tell my testimony about how everything magically changed and how happy I was as a perfect church girl. But even then, when I got my second chance, I was convinced I needed to keep my own slate clean. That's the kind of testimony you often hear, the one that resembles a makeover show with the "before and after" picture. "I used to be X, and now I'm Y."

Instead, I became a nervous wreck and arrogant performer who secretly graded everyone, most of all myself. It's the most miserable living, swearing you live for Jesus while being totally oblivious to who he really is.

FALSE ADVERTISING

Not long ago in my city of Guatemala a circuit of billboards showed up with big, fat letters that read, "YOU DON'T NEED GOD TO BE A GOOD PERSON." Wow. That's what we've reduced him to? A cosmic self-help guru? As a graphic designer, I know a little about advertising, and if atheists are going to invest in billboards, they're going to offer a direct countermessage to what they know Christians believe and say. Obviously I wasn't alone in assuming that the whole point of following God is self-improvement.

Now I understand what was happening: I really didn't want a relationship with Jesus. I wanted what I had seen "advertised"—a nifty Christian life—which is definitely not the same. Slowly but surely, though, my heart is now being led to love something better. I notice my joys have changed, and so have my sorrows. Because Someone fought a fierce battle to win my heart. Thankfully, he is so different from what I had fooled myself to believe.

That's why Jesus told the parables recorded in Luke 15, because my mess is the most common and the most

"MAKE NO MISTAKE: BEHAVIOR ONLY CHANGES PROFOUNDLY WHEN THE HEART IS CAPTIVATED."

dangerous. He uses a coin, a sheep, and a son to reveal our complete inability to even know we're lost and his total commitment to find those he set out to love. In all three stories we see a protagonist anguished over loss: The woman who sweeps her house and kneels and moves the furniture to find her little treasure. The shepherd whose heart pounds hard for the one who might be eaten by the wolves. And the dad whose loving character welcomes his wayward son back home to safety.

> But when he came to himself, he said, "How many of my father's hired servants have more than enough bread, but I perish here with hunger. I will arise and go to my father, and I will say to him, 'Father, I have sinned against heaven and before you. I am no longer worthy to be called your son. Treat me as one of your hired servants.'" (Luke 15:17–19)

This son didn't come to himself by self-examination, by gathering willpower, or by making another New Year's resolution. Sitting there hopeless with an empty belly, his cheeks were probably the only spot on his body not covered by smelly dry mud thanks to his cleansing tears. He remembered his dad's warm smile and gentle eyes, his hard-working hands, the smell of his robe, and the way he respectfully and lovingly instructed his staff. He could have treated these workers coldly or distantly, but they got fair treatment and generous daily doses of peace and protection. He came to himself by replaying in his mind what he knew was true: his father's character.

Make no mistake: Behavior only changes profoundly (not temporarily or superficially) when the heart is captivated. This son got a clear picture of his darkness and ungratefulness to the point of being humbled only because the amazing light of his father shone brighter in his current circumstances. Entitlement had been pulverized along with the riches he squandered. *Now* he was ready to go home. Hunger, peril, or shame can initially attract many, but only a clear picture of who the Father is and who we are will transform the affections and eventually the behavior.

This young wreck didn't get lost when he took the money to go to Las Vegas. Las Vegas revealed how lost he had always been. Resources and circumstances only highlight what commands you, what you truly hope in, and whom you really love. It's a blessing to get what you wanted and then discover that it's not enough, because you weren't designed to belong to it. Relationship saved that son, and it still saves. It takes this "aha" moment to bring you to your senses and realize you've been sleeping in a pigpen all along.

We lack the power to even know we need him or how far away from home we've wandered until he arrives with light and a map. That's exactly why the older son, the one the parable is actually written for, has such a hard time "coming to himself." I think that's why we don't get to see an explicit resolution in his case, because Jesus wanted to drag us into the story. I was the young one filled with obviously derailed affections, but I was also that begrudging older son who worked hard for the wrong reasons. And so are you. The older son was also lost, resenting his father, hoping to gain a favor that was already gladly granted. He was that arrogant performer who secretly graded everyone, beginning with himself. He lived the most miserable life, working for his dad while being totally oblivious to who he really was, drooling over the benefits and missing out on the true joy of a good father.

WE THREW A PARTY

So I take refuge in what I'm being taught by my teacher, Ms. Adoption. I am absolutely flawed, and so is my husband. What holds us together as a family on difficult days is not our children's performance. What holds us together is that we committed to love them before they even realized they were ours. We planned, saved, dreamed, shopped, visited doctors, worried, prayed for each of our children—biological and adopted—while they were completely unaware. In adoption, the relationship starts and is sustained by the ones who start it.

Remember me marching downstairs? In Luke 15 God marches down to see us, only without any mean butterflies and selfish motives. He tells us, "Son, you are always with me, and all that is mine is yours." In Jesus, the Father reaches out to the lost, but he can only bring back the ones who know they need to be found.

Some days my two little ones wish they hadn't been adopted. I know because they've told me, either with their words or with their actions. I'd be lying if I said it doesn't hurt, but I think of this: Before I ever marched downstairs in anger or suspicion, our family threw a party. We cried with relief when we brought our children home, because the healing process could begin. Their bed was a safe place, and their new names meant a new destiny. We threw them a party before they could rejoice with full understanding.

The dad in Luke 15 threw a party too. Not only because this child came back but also because of how he came back: with a truly sorrowful heart, aware of his wicked joys and selfish ways, grateful for his father's character. What brought that son back will now keep that son home. The party is thrown at the beginning, because he already knows the ending. His love will finally win the fierce battle for the hearts he set out to capture.

There will come a day when our laughter will make a million butterflies take flight in heaven. The ones you get when you're in love.

NEITHER SIN NOR SATAN NOR TWISTED SISTER COULD SNATCH ME FROM HIS HANDS

BY JEFF ROBINSON

" I WAS A CHRISTIAN, BUT I WAS OUT OF CHURCH, INTENTIONALLY CUT OFF FROM THE MEANS OF GRACE THAT NOURISH A BABY CHRISTIAN INTO MATURE ADULTHOOD. "

I t was a shame-inducing moment, one I had coming, but one God used as embers that would eventually grow into a flame of spiritual awakening.

I was a 21-year-old sports journalist and college student working for a daily newspaper in the Atlanta area, not far from my hometown in the north Georgia mountains. I arrived to cover the baseball game just moments before the first pitch. It was Sunday afternoon. As I hustled to prepare my scorecard and situate my pre-internet-era laptop and other implements, a colleague took his seat next to mine in the press box. I was wearing a coat and tie—atypical attire for watching a baseball game in the Peach State in July.

"Man, why are you so dressed up?" he asked. "You look like

you've been to church or something."

"I have been to church," I said. "I went to worship service this morning at First Baptist."

He looked confused. "Huh? That's a shocker. I've never taken you for the religious kind. You mean you're a Christian? I've never seen that in you."

His words, spoken matter-of-factly, left me feeling as if I'd grabbed onto a high-voltage wire. I spent all nine innings of that game thinking more about hypocrisy than homers. My Christian witness had taken a called third strike. Actually, it had never left the dugout. I was humiliated, not because he had failed to see some piety in me, but because my life didn't match what he rightly expected to see from a follower of Jesus Christ. That day was the first time I had been to church in three years. He was right; there was no evidence that I was a Christian.

But it hadn't always been that way.

Like many Southern Baptist youth of my generation, I grew up in church, made a profession of faith at 10, and followed the Lord until age 17. My family was in church Sunday morning, Sunday night, Monday night, Tuesday night, and Wednesday night. I was an officer in Fellowship of Christian Athletes, a leader in my youth group, and a mediocre but eager singer in youth choir. But the summer before my senior year of high school, my affections began to change. My heart grew cold toward Jesus and his church. When I graduated from youth group, I left church too.

A private detective couldn't have located my Bible.

I began to go places no Christian should. I hung out with people whose rebellion didn't trouble their consciences. I had friends in low places. I joined a rock band; this was the mid-'80s, the so-called "decade of excess," so you know what that meant. For a number of years, I lived the rock lifestyle. Jesus was out. Judas Priest was in.

Though my time in the band was somewhat short-lived, my time as a prodigal was not. If being a Christian would've been a crime, no honest judge would've found me guilty. I was a Christian, but I was out of church, intentionally cut off from the means of grace that nourish a baby Christian into mature adulthood.

AFTER DARKNESS, LIGHT

Mercifully, the hound of heaven trailed me in the middle of my rebellion. I sinned boldly, but I didn't enjoy a nanosecond of it. The Spirit of God convicted me time and again. One night I returned home from a bar in Athens, Georgia, and lay awake all night sweating, thinking about the reality of hell, hearing Jesus's words in Matthew 13:50: "and throw them into the blazing furnace, where there will be weeping and wailing and gnashing of teeth." Other Scripture verses—learned in vacation Bible school, youth group, and in my home—warred with my mind for months on end.

One night I awoke in a sweat from a nightmare that I was being dragged to hell by a satanic minion dressed like a black-hooded executioner. During a rock concert in Atlanta, I had told a friend, "We really shouldn't be here. The things we're doing aren't right." He thought I needed another beer. I needed to come home to Jesus—and I knew it.

Thirty years later, I'm convinced God was at work in my heart. Eventually, through a series of personal and biblical conversations with my older brother, my parents, and our pastor, the Lord drew me back to himself. He granted me repentance that left me weeping for days over my sin, then rejoicing for months over the burden of guilt being lifted. At 22, the prodigal had returned to his Father.

But what happened? Did I lose my salvation during my late teenage years, only to regain it as a young adult? Some might think so. I don't. Scripture is clear that nothing can pluck a genuine believer from the hand of God (John 10:27–29)—not sin, not Satan, not Twisted Sister.

As I believe my experience shows, it's possible for a genuine Christian to sin grievously, to spend a season away from the Lord, and later return—found by the Father while lost and wandering in a remote country. Scripture demonstrates this view, particularly in the profound contrast between two men who walked closely with Jesus: Peter and Judas.

TALE OF TWO APOSTATES

Peter was one of God's choice servants. But he was also a bit of a character. So zealous (and sometimes misguided) was he for the Savior, Peter cut off a soldier's ear when he realized they had arrived to arrest Jesus. But Peter's devotion was inconsistent. Yes, he could be bold. But he could also be rash, petulant, even unwise and fearful. On the night of the Lord's crucifixion, he denied Jesus—not once, not twice, but three times—even cowering at the feet of a preteen girl who accused him of being a follower of Christ.

In the shadow of violent Calvary, Peter wanted nothing to do with Jesus. But God was by no means finished with Peter. Our Lord interceded for him (Luke 22:32). Peter was restored (John 21:15–19), wrote two books of the New Testament, and preached as the Spirit came in his fullness at Pentecost. Tradition says he ultimately laid down his life for the cause of Christ—being crucified upside down because he considered himself unworthy to be put to death in the same manner as Jesus. Peter was lost, but because he was one of Christ's sheep, God found him.

Peter's transformation illustrates many important lessons. Perhaps chief among them is that you don't truly find yourself until you lose yourself for the sake of Christ. Peter spent three years in Jesus's orbit, yet he neither understood his Savior nor the demands of following him. But God's grace was greater than Peter's foolishness. Peter encountered the risen Savior at the end of John's Gospel (John 22) where he was famously restored—the Lord asking Peter three times (once for each denial) if he loved his Lord. Peter had failed—big time—and he didn't repent in the way we usually expect. Scripture doesn't indicate any act of repentance from Peter before he heard of Jesus's resurrection and ran to the tomb. Yet Jesus graciously restored him. Thankfully, being reconciled to God does not depend on summoning enough strength to repent, but on Christ welcoming us by his grace.

My story bears some similarities. I attended church regularly for nearly two decades, had heard the gospel hundreds of times, and had even embraced it as my own. Yet I was clueless about the cost of following Jesus—that discipleship demands my life, my soul, my all. My faith was weak, but, like Peter, Jesus found me through a set of providential circumstances when I wasn't really looking for him.

Following Jesus comes at a high cost, but I didn't always live as if that were true. Over decades, God's grace grew me into a disciple willing to forsake everything for Jesus.

It was the same with Peter. Peter the chicken-hearted became Peter the lion-hearted. Our faith may be weak at times, hut the object of our faith is not. God never changes. Yes, Peter was utterly unworthy of grace when he denied his Lord. I was unworthy of grace when I chased hard after the world. But grace is just that—favor unmerited. Jesus did for Peter and me what we could never do for ourselves. I turned away for a while. Peter did the same. But Christ called us home.

By contrast, think of Judas. Praise the Lord I didn't turn out to be a Judas—a false follower of Christ. He traveled with Jesus nearly as long as Peter did, yet he betrayed the Lord into the hands of the authorities. Jesus called Judas the "son of perdition" who fell away as prophesied by Scripture (John 17:12).

We often overlook that while Peter initially showed no remorse for denying Jesus, Judas actually did show remorse for betraying Jesus. Matthew 27:3–5 details Judas's anguish:

> Then when Judas, his betrayer, saw that Jesus was condemned, he changed his mind and brought back the thirty pieces of silver to the chief priests and the elders, saying, "I have sinned by betraying innocent blood." They said, "What is that to us? See to it yourself." And throwing down the pieces of silver into the temple, he departed, and he went and hanged himself.

Judas showed remorse, but not genuine repentance after he sinned against his friend Jesus. Judas didn't even try to defend Jesus against the dubious accusations. He just sought to salve his conscience by returning the blood money. Ultimately, Judas took his own life at the end of a rope rather than face his crushing guilt and seek forgiveness.

GENUINE REPENTANCE AND SELFISH REMORSE

As we see in Peter and Judas, Scripture expresses two drastically different responses to the realization of our sin. The apostle Paul wrote in 2 Corinthians 7:10, "For godly grief produces a repentance that leads to salvation without regret, whereas worldly grief produces death."

First, there is "worldly grief," which is being sorry for getting caught. It says, "I'm sorry if I offended you. I'm sorry I made myself look bad." Godly grief, by contrast, says, "I'm sorry I sinned. It says I'm sorry I offended a holy God and broke his law. I'm sorry I made God look bad." Judas's worldly grief produced death. Peter, on the other hand, showed godly grief. He went on to become one of the most powerful followers of Christ. His zeal for Christ is unquestioned. The man who once denied Christ would lose his life for the sake of Christ.

Two parables in Luke 15:1–10 depict Jesus as going after the one lost lamb, the one lost coin. This is the way Jesus worked with Peter. This is grace. He restored Peter after his wandering. It was the same with me. Peter blew it, and I blew it, but God's grace was greater still.

As a pastor I'm often asked how a disciple of Christ can fall prey to the unholy trinity of the world, the flesh, and the Devil. "Doesn't the fact that they still sin mean they aren't really Christians after all?" I'm sometimes asked. But genuine Christians will still struggle against sin until they die and go to Jesus, or until he returns. Their journey of faith may take a detour for a time. But a genuine follower of Christ will persevere to the end, by the power of the Spirit.

I spent years looking for love in all the wrong places. But the love of Jesus found me, even when I seemed lost in a fog of competing desires, some of them destructive. Our great (and only) hope is Jesus, as George Matheson gloriously reminds us in his great hymn:

O Love that will not let me go
I rest my weary soul in thee
I give thee back the life I owe
That in thine ocean depths its flow
May richer, fuller be.

I BELIEVE IN SUCCESS

▬

BY JASON COOK

"HOW CAN I BE SUCCESSFUL IN THIS LIFE AND THE NEXT?"

believe success matters. I believe it matters because it's the message we receive from our earliest years. If you behave well, your behavior will be rewarded. If you behave poorly, your behavior will be punished.

I believe in success because we're evangelized through the tales we hear. Every story essentially follows the same plot. The cast is introduced, an antagonist arrives on the scene, and shortly thereafter a problem arises. The narrative creeps to the climax as the tension builds. The protagonist defeats the antagonist, and the day is won. The hero succeeds.

I believe success matters because we are inundated with

images of success. Courses offer plans to build your net worth. Cultural icons display their latest project for the world. Business tycoons share their rags-to-riches stories. We see lavish lifestyles and desire that success. Social media are littered with the life you should be living, your best life now. And you can arrive there by surrounding yourself with the people and things that make you successful.

I believe success matters because of how it makes us feel. Carpenters know the sense of pride that comes from taming a piece of wood and creating something useful. Artisans know the meaning that comes from molding stubborn materials into functional and often beautiful instruments for admiration.

I believe success matters because the multi-billion-dollar sports industry tells us. We applaud and admire champions. We loathe losers. We remember the greats and legends. We forget the bad-news bears. Hero worship is so ingrained in culture that children emulate the batting stances, jump shots, and fashion choices of their heroes. Who am I kidding? I still emulate the iconic batting stance and pose of Ken Griffey Jr. after he belted one into the right-field bleachers.

I believe success matters.

And if the rich young man could speak with us today, he'd agree.

If we need a picture of success in the New Testament we should look no further than this man (Luke 18:18–30). He's extremely wealthy and possesses ruling power to complete the one-two combo of success. Whether he inherited his fortune or amassed it himself, we don't know. But he came to Jesus with a question it would appear his fortune couldn't answer. It's a question that revealed discontent in his heart. The question appeared earnest. But this text invites us to dig deeper to find the core motivation behind the age-old question: "Good Teacher, what must I do to inherit eternal life?" To put it another way, "How can I be successful in this life and the next?"

It's a great question. It's an earnest question. It's an ultimate question. Surely this rich and powerful man should know the answer.

His first word—*good*—signaled how his encounter with Jesus would end.

Goodness, in the New Testament sense, carries a dual understanding of obedience to the law and pure motivation of the heart. For someone to be good, he or she must uphold the law perfectly and have a pure heart while doing so. Scripture often reminds us that no man is "good" (Eccles. 7:10; Ps. 14:3; Isa. 64:6; Rom. 3:10–12; Eph. 2:1–3). As revealed in this encounter with Jesus, the young man was neither good in his ardent obedience nor in his motivations. Had the rich young man heard the Sermon on the Mount, he would have understood this problem. Many Pharisees believed if they weren't committing adultery—even if they were burning with lust—then they preserved their righteousness (Matt. 5:27–28). Likewise with murder (Matt. 5:21–22). You could secretly hate and despise another, but without physically taking a life you could uphold the law. Jesus obliterated this understanding by cutting to the core of the law: pure obedience *and* pure motivation. Not only should you not commit adultery; even one drop of lust makes you unrighteous. Not only should you not murder; even one drop of hatred in your heart means you've picked up the knife and committed the action. No one is good. Only God.

Jesus challenged his idea of goodness to reveal his misunderstanding. The rich young man asked Jesus what he must "do" to inherit eternal life, and Jesus answered in kind. He provided a list of things to to perform. And the young man responded without blushing, "All these I have kept from my youth." But the arrogant response revealed a self-centered view of obedience. Not only had he overestimated his faithfulness to the law, his heart wasn't pure. He fully believed he was good. Had he stopped long enough to consider Jesus's question of goodness, he may have realized that no man is good. No, not one. Neither in deed nor in motivation.

I resonate with this man. For I, too, was once driven by the need to "do" something in order to earn salvation.

"HIS MONEY COULDN'T BUY HIM THE ONE THING HE SO EARNESTLY DESIRED: A RELATIONSHIP WITH GOD THAT LED TO ETERNAL LIFE."

I TRIED, I FAILED

Having been raised in a Word of Faith offshoot of the charismatic tradition, my spiritual life was, in part, a product of the prosperity gospel. My prayer life was mostly pleas and requests for earthly comforts. Around 7 years of age I remember praying that God would give me $20, because I knew not having enough money was the product of secret sin, lack of faith, or a failure to love God completely. And as much as I loved God, I still did not have any money. All of my childhood pastors were successful men. They wore $10,000 suits, drove beautiful cars, and inhabited sprawling estates. They lived in opulence that I desired and could have if I just followed the plan of blessing they laid out. And so I did. Or at least I tried. I would confidently pray with faith in the power of God, I would boldly speak things into existence, and I made sure to walk in "perfection" so as to not forfeit my blessing. I did this for years with little success. The plans they laid out didn't work for me. What began as strong affection for Christ in my teens was supplanted with suspicion, disillusionment, and bitterness in my college years. My pastors told me that God called us to be perfect. And I tried.

Yet no matter how much I tried, I failed. I failed in accruing material success, and I lacked any true assurance of faith. Petitions for salvation frequently went up on Sunday mornings. There I could receive some absolution from a week of sinful frivolity. Church became the cleansing bath before I walked out into the world and got dirty again. I tried to convince myself that I was a good man doing good things. But through those years of "doing," I had made no progress in being materially successful or knowing with certainty my eternal forever home. I had only succeeded in "doing" poorly.

And if I performed poorly, then I could not be loved. That was the unspoken message I learned from a culture of success. It was the message I heard preached in church. And it was the message I lived by on the football field. When you play well, you receive recognition and admiration that is difficult to rival. Play poorly and you'll rue the day you laced up your cleats.

During my entire career I knew that love was predicated on my performance. So, even if my relationship with God was rocky, I could be loved by adoring fans—so long as we won games. Armed with this thinking, I built my entire life around the ideas of success and performance at the highest levels. As a football player the highest level of success is the NFL, and I made it. I performed well. But even on top of the world, I didn't feel deeply loved. I was sad. I didn't feel any more loved by God. Even the biggest stage in my profession was insufficient. I still felt worthless. A deep shame came over me as I considered that I had built my life around a lie. Feeling this failure, I began to wrestle with God. Specifically I began to wrestle with the message of salvation I had been taught. I realized I had made the same grave error as the rich young man: I was worshiping a different god.

> When Jesus heard this, he said to him, "One thing you still lack. Sell all that you have and distribute to the poor, and you will have treasure in heaven; and come, follow me." But when he heard these things, he became very sad, for he was extremely rich. (Matt. 5:22–23)

Why did Jesus respond to the young man's arrogant response this way? It was a test of the first commandment. A test the man had failed. In all his earthly success and perceived spiritual success, his money couldn't buy him the one thing he so earnestly desired: a relationship with God that led to eternal life. Money was the rich young man's god, his idol. And in making money an idol, he violated the first commandment of God: "You shall have no other gods before me." Jesus didn't want his money. Jesus wanted his heart. Sadness came over him as he pondered the loss of this god.

The rich young man lacked true dependence on the grace of God for eternal life. Had he stopped long enough to consider the meaning of "good" he would have seen that Jesus is good. Had he paused to consider the law he would have realized the impotence of his goodness and futility of his self-righteousness. In lacking dependence on the grace of God, this wealthy man found himself in spiritual poverty. A successful man relegated to failure.

It's interesting that Jesus told him to give his money away to the poor. The writer, Luke, contrasted wealth and poverty throughout his Gospel. His recording of the Beatitudes from Jesus is a prime example: "Blessed are you who are poor, for yours is the kingdom of God. Blessed are you who hunger now, for you will be satisfied" (Luke 6:20–21). He extended the contrast three verses later by juxtaposing the estate of the rich. "But woe to you who are rich, for you have already received your comfort. Woe to you who are well fed now, for you will go hungry" (Luke 6:24–25). Luke intentionally showcased those materially poor and poor in spirit as nearer to the kingdom of God, while giving stern warnings to the affluent. One waits in anguish for the comforts of a coming kingdom; the other lives in comfort now but will reap anguish in the kingdom to come.

What the poor lack, the rich young man possessed in material wealth. What the poor have, however, the rich young man lacked—humility. By ridding himself of material comforts and earthly props, he may have seen the vast wealth of the poor. By setting aside the incessant idol of self-reliance, he may have learned much from the poor. It's the quintessential biblical lesson of gaining by losing. Lose the life you've built around success and gain a satisfying relationship with Jesus. Forsaking this invitation, the rich young man left in sadness. Jesus made known to those who heard their exchange that it's exceedingly difficult for a rich person to get into heaven.

The crowd around Jesus apparently saw the wealthy as closer to God. When Jesus humorously noted the difficulty of wealthy individuals to enter into the kingdom, many around asked in shock, "Then who can be saved?" In this question and the ensuing response we discover the beauty of the gospel. The whole discourse has led to this moment. The rich young man's wealth can't save. His partial obedience to the law can't save. His refusal to exchange his love of money to follow Jesus has ended in sadness. No wonder those present audibly wonder, "If this model of success can't find salvation then who can?" Jesus answers, "What is impossible with man is possible with God."

NO OTHER HOPE

There is no hope outside the work of God in Christ on your behalf. Salvation for rich or for poor is always a miracle of God, always a gift of God. This is the good news of Jesus Christ. This message rescued me from effort-based righteousness. It rescued me from practicing Christianity without Christ. By faith in the finished work of Jesus, I found myself deeply loved. No assurance of eternal life was found in my own attempts. It was impossible. But what is impossible with man is possible with God.

When our earthly attempts to be spiritually successful fail, we find the answer to the question, "How can I earn eternal life?" In Christ alone, by faith alone, through grace alone.

I believe success matters. I believe it matters because Jesus successfully accomplished what I could not. And his grace is the key that unlocks the question of the rich young ruler.

From time to time I remember the days following my greatest success, and I'm reminded of Ephesians 2:4: "But God, being rich in mercy, because of the great love with which he loved us, even when we were dead in our trespasses, made us alive together with Christ—by grace you have been saved." Grace is the undeserved, unearned kindness of God. And this grace is never in short supply. If you've found that chasing your wildest dreams results in sadness, there is grace for you. If you've achieved your greatest aspirations, and they have been revealed for the ruse that earthly success is, there is grace for you. If you've been unsuccessful in finding true rest from your strivings for perfection, there is grace for you.

Or perhaps you still believe success will make people love you. You should know that only Jesus can be the hero to your story. Only in him is success always sure. I hope your every effort of winning through performance, every effort of self-justification, and every pursuit of accolades will fail. And in that failure, by faith, you'll find true success: resting in the finished work of Jesus.

That is the only success profitable in this life and also the life to come.

THE WORDS OF ETERNAL LIFE

BY SAM CHAN

—

"IN THE END, WHAT ARE WE REALLY LOOKING FOR IN LIFE?

ords give us meaning, purpose, and hope.

We hear it every day: "Do whatever makes you happy." These words are the unchallenged mantra of our times. Maybe they inspire you to get out of bed every day. Maybe they are the unofficial motto of your life.

But with all this advice to be happy, why are we so unhappy? With all this freedom to do whatever we want, why are we more anxious, stressed, and depressed than ever before?

If you meet me in real life, you'll see that I'm Asian. Short. And 51 years of age.

That last bit shocks most people, because they say that I don't (yet) look that old. But it also shocks me, because it means I've probably lived more years than I'm going to have left. It also means I've had enough time to see that our dreams and ambitions rarely go the way we'd hoped.

The first 25 years of my life went according to the Asian-immigrant high-achieving script. Study hard. Stay out of trouble. Get a degree. Become a doctor. It was an endless series of successes.

But the next 20 years did not go according to script. After working for four years as a doctor, I burned out. No problem, I thought, because I left it for a so-called higher calling into Christian ministry. But, after teaching for nine years in a seminary, that job also ended on a sour note. And now I was jaded, bitter, and disaffected by both secular *and* sacred professions.

So, five years ago, at the halfway point of life, I had to decide what I wanted to do.

At first, I thought I wanted to go *back* to medicine and finish my specialization. Become a surgeon. Surely that'd be the right thing. I would finish off a chapter in my life that had always nagged me.

Oh, to be a surgeon! Then I would have financial security. My kids could have a good education. Our family could enjoy overseas vacations. We'd have high social standing.

And I'd have the respect of my peers.

But my neighbor, who is a career adviser, looked me in the eye and asked, "*Why* do you want to be a surgeon?" And I couldn't answer him truthfully. Because I knew all of the above reasons were terrible reasons to become a surgeon.

It all goes back to the bigger questions of life. What am I looking for? What is the point of life anyway?

Is it to be successful? That's what my parents' generation was told. So they got their degrees, got their jobs, and bought their houses. But they found that life empty and unfulfilling. And so that would be me, as a surgeon, with my cars, social standing, and houses.

Is it to be happy? Because that's what our present generation is being told. But this view is making us more stressed, more tired, more miserable. Because "happiness" is an unachievable goal. By looking for it, you're guaranteed *not* to find it. And that would be me, as a surgeon, with my overseas vacations.

In the end, what are we really looking for in life? I believe it's a combination of validation and fulfillment.

The first thing we seek is validation. Many of my friends are parents whose children have grown up and left home. And now my friends are left with the nagging doubt that they could've done better as parents when their children were younger. But it's too late. The children have grown up. Moved out. And now my friends look at me and say, "All we want is for our children to tell us that we did okay as parents. But they never do."

Maybe we try to find validation in our work. Get our qualifications. Get our promotions. Get the corner office. But the problem is, once you reach the top, there's no one up there to tell you that you've done well. I once caught up with a friend. We'd trained together as junior doctors. But whereas my medical career went nowhere, he was now a respected and successful surgeon. I innocently asked, "They tell me it's lonely at the top. Is that true?" He looked at me and painfully said, "It is so true."

We crave validation from those closest to us. But the sad irony of life is many of us will never hear the words we crave. Thousands of "likes" and "congrats!" from friends we barely know on Facebook will not suffice.

The second thing we look for in life is fulfillment. This one is even trickier. To be fulfilled is to have achieved the goal of your mission. The mission of an acorn is to become an oak tree, Aristotle said. So, when an acorn becomes that oak tree, it is *fulfilled*. It has attained a *full life*. Likewise, if we want fulfillment, we need to know our mission in life. But doesn't that just bring us back to where we started? We can't have fulfillment if we don't know the point of life! We can't have a full life if we don't know what to fill it with.

So where can we find validation and fulfillment?

TURNING POINT

I believe part of the answer comes in the story from John 6:60–69. This is a turning point in the life of Jesus. Up until now, Jesus has performed many miracles. He has turned water into wine, walked on water, and cured a man who'd been unable to walk for 38 years. But his most recent miracle has been the most spectacular. He miraculously produced, from five small loaves, enough bread to feed more than 5,000 people.

As a result, crowds of people are following Jesus. They love his teachings. They love his miracles and healings. But they especially love that he gave them so much bread. If Jesus keeps doing this, they're guaranteed a life of security, provision, and health.

But Jesus now says something that turns many away. After this, only a small handful will stay behind to follow Jesus.

"The Spirit gives life; the flesh counts for nothing. The words I have spoken to you—they are full of the Spirit and life" (John 6:63).

If I were in the crowds that day, I would've found this bit especially offensive: "the flesh counts for nothing." Jesus is saying that everything we've chased after in life—success, happiness, pleasures, health, a stable income—counts for *nothing*.

But how can these good things count for nothing? I hope my children will have success, happiness, pleasures, health, and a stable income. I certainly wouldn't wish the opposite on them—failures, sadness, pains, diseases, and bankruptcy! So why does Jesus say that they count for nothing?

Because they're nothing in comparison with the Spirit who gives life.

In other words, it's not that the crowds wanted too much from Jesus. They wanted too little. Jesus wanted to give them more—the Spirit who gives life. But they only wanted Jesus to give them bread.

And we might be like the crowds. Just like they became obsessed with bread, so we become obsessed with the material things in life—financial security, job success, six-pack abs, and a ski holiday in Vail. These are good things, but they mustn't become ultimate things. In his book *The Happiness Hypothesis*, Jonathan Haidt writes about the futility of our striving. For all who believe the next car or vacation or bonus will satisfy them, there will always be a newer car, longer vacation, and bigger bonus just beyond their grasp.

If the good things of this life are all we're looking for, then we're selling ourselves short. They're nothing in comparison with what Jesus can give us. Just like the crowds, we also need the Spirit who gives life.

WORDS OF JESUS

But how can we find this Spirit who gives life? By knowing the Spirit-giver himself: Jesus. And how do we do this? By believing his *words*.

This is why Jesus says his "words" are full of Spirit and life. And that's why Simon Peter decides to be loyal to Jesus, because he alone has the "words of eternal life."

So our two basic choices in life are these:

(1) Be true to yourself. Only we can tell ourselves what to do. David Brooks writes about this option in his book *The Road to Character*. He quotes the philosopher Charles Taylor, who notes that this choice assumes that inside all of us is a "Golden Figure." We need to ignore all other forms of authority. Only we can be our moral compass. Our goal is to be authentic—to embrace and express the true self inside me.

or

(2) Be true to someone or something else. We're repeatedly told the first option is the only choice. But, more and more, we're realizing that we should choose the second, as countercultural and counterintuitive as it first appears.

Viktor Frankl, a Holocaust survivor, tells a parable in his book *Man's Search for Meaning*. Imagine we know two women. The first is blessed with good looks, riches, and success. At the end of her life, she may say, "Huh! What was the point of it all? I went to parties. I flirted with men. I was rich. But, really, what was all that about?"

The second woman has the opposite fortune. She gives birth to a child of profound disabilities. For the rest of her life, she sacrifices her life to raise and nurture this child. But, at the end of her life, she may say, "Wow. How about that? I just raised a child with profound disabilities."

In other words, the first woman finds that pleasures and successes, by themselves, are self-focused, empty, and unfulfilling. But the second woman discovers that serving someone else is deeply rich and fulfilling.

Frankl concludes that, although we shouldn't look for suffering and failures, they will find us. They're an inevitable part of life. We become who we are because of them. And more than that, the purpose of life is to live for someone else. Someone bigger than ourselves. A bigger story than just our own story.

And that is exactly what Jesus offers. He's the ultimate Somebody to live for. His story is bigger than our own. If we live for him, we'll find a fulfilled life. A full life. Or, as Jesus calls it, eternal life.

So, there I was, five years ago, at the halfway point of life, facing the same two choices. I could re-enter the pathway to becoming a surgeon. I could chase the riches and pleasures promised by that career. *I owe it to myself*, I thought. *After all, hadn't I done enough sacrificing for others? It was time that I got to live for myself. How many years do I have left anyway? You only live once!* But, deep down, I knew that riches and pleasures, by themselves, would only make me more self-absorbed, empty, and unfulfilled. I was also too old! I had young children. It was the wrong stage of life to do something like this.

Ultimately, I knew that I needed something more—more than riches, pleasures, success, status, and security. I needed the words of Jesus.

And so I made a different choice. I decided to go into a job where I could give talks about Jesus to high schoolers, university students, lawyers, doctors, and city workers. This job would pay less. It would have less security. But it would be more fulfilling, because I'd be sharing the "words of eternal life."

I'm not saying that's what you should also do. But I am saying this: If Jesus really does have the words of eternal life, it will affect the big choices we make in life. At some stage, we'll face a similar dilemma. Will my life remain self-absorbed, empty, and ultimately unfulfilled? Or will my life be fulfilled—filled by Jesus and his words?

ATTRACTIVE OFFER

What does it mean to be filled by Jesus and his life-giving words?

Jesus's words give us the validation we crave. Jesus says to us, "I chose you" (John 15:16). "I have called you friends" (John 15:15). "I love you" (John 15:9). He doesn't promise us a life free from pain and suffering. In fact, he guarantees suffering if we follow him. But, through all of it, we know he is with us. And he validates us by loving us, dying for us, and living for us.

Jesus's words also give us the fulfillment that we need. Ultimately, the goal of life is to love and worship our Creator. To be connected to him. To be part of his bigger story for us. Thus, if we believe Jesus's words, then we will know Jesus. And we will have a fulfilled life.

When we read about Jesus in the Bible, many things amaze us. He taught with authority. He went against the conventions of his time. His miracles and healings were spectacular. His love, compassion, and kindness were unprecedented. No wonder crowds happily followed wherever he went.

But if that's all we're taking away from Jesus, then, just like the crowds, we're selling ourselves short. Jesus wants to give us more. He wants to give us eternal life.

On the one hand, this is an attractive offer. Who doesn't want eternal life? But, on the other hand, it's a confronting offer. Because Jesus is also saying that whatever we're living for right now will ultimately be unfulfilling. Do we react with disgust, especially because we've already invested so much into our lives? Or can we humble ourselves enough to say, "You know what? It's about time I admitted that my life is self-absorbed, empty, and unfulfilling. Up until now, I've followed the prescribed path of living for myself, but to be honest, it hasn't delivered what was promised."

So what does Jesus promise us instead? Hardships. Suffering. But also the "words of eternal life."

If our lives are filled by Jesus, his Spirit, and his words, then our lives will be *filled*. A full life. A fulfilled life. Everlasting life.

FROM BAR MITZVAH TO BAPTISM

BY BERNARD N. HOWARD

"IS JESUS THE JEWISH MESSIAH?"

Officer to cadet: "I didn't see you at camouflage training today."

Cadet to officer: "Thank you, sir."

It's an old joke, but it's relevant to anyone thinking of becoming a Christian. True faith in Jesus makes it impossible to blend into the background. Believers can't avoid standing out, especially if they come from a culture that typically rejects Christianity, such as my own Jewish culture.

My encounter with Jesus began when two boys at my high school made an announcement at morning assembly. They said a visiting speaker was coming to the school's Christian group, and they encouraged anyone who wanted to learn more about Jesus to come along. Their announcement caught my attention, because for two years I'd been asking myself whether life had any meaning or point to it.

LIFTED UP

At the start of that search for meaning, when I was 13, I'd had my Bar Mitzvah, the Jewish coming-of-age ceremony. Outwardly, everything had gone smoothly. I'd recited a portion of the Hebrew Bible to a synagogue full of supportive people. But the preparation process hadn't answered my big questions about life: *Why am I here? Is there a God, and, if so, how can I be sure he exists? What's the point of life if we all end up buried and forgotten?*

That last question particularly gnawed at me. Life seemed like writing a book using a special ink that will one day fade into nothingness. Why write the book if the ink will disappear? Why throw yourself into life, with its hopes and sweat and tears of sadness or joy, when death will make it all meaningless? I was hunting for answers, and so when the boys advertised their Christian group, I thought it was worth a try.

The guest speaker gave a talk on one sentence from the Bible: "As Moses lifted up the serpent in the wilderness, so must the Son of Man be lifted up, that whoever believes in him may have eternal life" (John 3:14–15).

The speaker, a pastor named Jonathan Fletcher, said this teaching meant that when Jesus was lifted up on the cross, he made it possible for people to live forever. Jonathan explained that when the Israelites were in the wilderness, they were plagued by venomous snakes (Num. 21:6–8). Moses fixed a bronze snake to a pole, and he told the Israelites that if they were bitten, they could look at the snake on the pole, and they would live (Num. 21:9). Jonathan said our wrongdoing is more serious in God's eyes than a lethal snakebite. But Jesus was willingly nailed to the cross to solve that problem by receiving the punishment for other people's sin. All we need do is look and live.

I knew immediately that eternal life would transform everything for me. But one matter still had to be addressed. I went to Jonathan after the talk and said, "I'm Jewish, so I suppose this isn't for me." He replied, "Jesus himself is Jewish! He's the Jewish Messiah, the one the Jews were waiting for. If you follow him, you'll be following your own Messiah." It was extremely reassuring to hear that I could still be Jewish and believe in Jesus. I began following Jesus that evening and gratefully received the gift of eternal life.

STICKING OUT

Although I was persuaded that I could hold on to my Jewishness while following Jesus, other Jewish people weren't so sure. This is where that joke about camouflage training comes in. When a Jewish person starts following Jesus, it's no longer possible to blend in with the Jewish community. There have always been Jewish followers of Jesus—in fact, right at the start, *all* his followers were Jewish—but most Jewish people don't accept Jesus's claim to be the Messiah. So I knew that by becoming a Jewish believer in Jesus I would inevitably stick out. The same is true in other cultures. In most parts of the world, people who become Christians know that following Jesus will separate them in various ways from the crowd.

Jesus himself gave us an example of courageously standing out. When he declared himself to be the long-awaited Messiah, he was putting his life at stake. In the hearing of the religious leaders of the time, he said these haunting words:

> O Jerusalem, Jerusalem, the city that kills the prophets and stones those who are sent to it! How often would I have gathered your children together as a hen gathers her brood under her wings, and you were not willing! See, your house is left to you desolate. For I tell you, you will not see me again, until you say, "Blessed is he who comes in the name of the Lord." (Matt. 23:37–39)

It's a speech full of darkness, until a small circle of light shows up at the tunnel's end.

Jesus spoke of the deaths of prophets in ancient times, slain by a city unwilling to hear their message. His hearers knew their city's history, and they would have agreed that terrible things had happened there in the past. But then Jesus revealed that the pattern was about to be repeated. He said the city had refused to allow him to gather its people to him. Jerusalem had rejected his claim to be the Messiah—God's promised king. He knew he was about to receive the same treatment as those prophets killed in the past. And yet since he truly *is* God's Messiah, his absence would leave the city desolate, not only lacking its appointed ruler but also responsible for his death.

Talk about standing out from the crowd! Jesus was speaking to men serving as the leaders of God's chosen people. He was telling them that he is their true king, and by rejecting him they would bring desolation on themselves. These men, who saw themselves as pillars among God's people, were lost despite thinking they were found.

Then the bright circle of hope appeared. Jesus said the city would see him again, and at that time it would welcome him as God's chosen king. But the only people who would share in that glorious eternity are those who accept that he is the One sent by God, the One who "comes in the name of the Lord." It's a prophecy that makes sense if you factor in Jesus's resurrection from the dead, his ascension to heaven, and his future return.

The implication for Jesus's Jewish hearers on that day—and ultimately, all humanity—is clear. To see Jesus installed in Jerusalem as God's eternal king, and to enjoy his perfect rule forever, we need to acknowledge him as the One he says he is. And we need to do so whatever the short-term costs might be in this life—such as the pain of no longer fitting in.

CONTROVERSY ERUPTS

One of the things that makes it so hard to stick out is that the group usually thinks it has everything under control. When someone pursues a radically different agenda, it's a challenge to that status quo—a challenge that is easier to crush than take to heart.

This challenge became real for me in college when I helped arrange an outreach event titled "Is Jesus the Jewish Messiah?" As the title suggests, it was primarily aimed at my fellow Jewish students. I wanted them to hear the same good news about eternal life that I'd been so thrilled to encounter at high school. But a local rabbi named Shmuley Boteach (who, strangely enough, later became a spiritual adviser to Michael Jackson) found out about the event and strenuously objected to it.

Rabbi Boteach went on record with a statement about our event: "I thought we were in the age of mutual understanding and respect, not the age of spiritual Nazism whereby one faith is promoted as being superior to another or where an ancient people are targeted for conversion by small-minded bigots." The statement was so fiercely worded that it made it into the student newspaper and then into one or two national papers as well. A radio breakfast show invited the rabbi and me to debate each other in its studio. Everyone advised me not to accept (due to my lack of experience), and my pastor kindly agreed to take my side of the debate.

While the storm was raging, I had plenty of adrenaline to see me through. But afterward I found out that the news had reached my grandmother, among other members of my family. I'd been waiting for the right time to tell her about my faith in Jesus, but the controversial outreach event made that decision for me. For many years she didn't even want to see me or talk to me, and things between us only ever got slightly better in the last few years of her life.

My parents were much more understanding, although they did ask me to postpone my baptism. So instead of joining in as planned at a river baptism with several others from my church, I was baptized later that year at a Christian summer camp.

In the eyes of the Jewish community, baptism is often

seen as a renunciation of Jewishness. But I viewed it as a way to follow in the footsteps of Jesus the Jewish Messiah, who was himself baptized at the start of his ministry by his (Jewish) cousin John. Baptism makes a person's membership of the Christian community public and official. Although it can have the effect of separating Jewish believers in Jesus from their family and friends, it has a wonderful upside. Joining the Christian community means gaining a new family.

This is something Jesus pointed out when Peter, one of his followers, said, "We have left everything to follow you!" In reply, Jesus promised that anyone who follows him would have a hundred times as many family members even in this life:

> Truly, I say to you, there is no one who has left house or brothers or sisters or mother or father or children or lands, for my sake and for the gospel, who will not receive a hundredfold now in this time, houses and brothers and sisters and mothers and children and lands, with persecutions, and in the age to come eternal life. (Mark 10:29–31; see also Mark 3:31–35)

These words aren't the overflowing idealism of a religious leader. In my experience, they've proved to be true time and time again.

Manhattan, where I live and work as the pastor of a small

church, is a place where it's easy to be anonymous in the midst of millions. Of course, a kind of camaraderie develops among office co-workers, but when the axe falls and a newly unemployed Manhattanite is gathering personal belongings into a cardboard box, many in the room will simply look away. That's never the case at church. The sense of community at our Sunday meeting and midweek evening meal is palpable, and the word "family" seems perfectly appropriate. While following Jesus can mean losing biological family members, it also means finding a family with an eternal bond.

FLYING THE COOP

Jesus's words to the religious leaders in Jerusalem, quoted earlier in this chapter, include a memorable image: "How often would I have gathered your children together as a hen gathers her brood under her wings, and you were not willing!" (Matt. 23:37).

If anyone thought they belonged to God's hen coop, it was Jesus's hearers on that day: Pharisees and scribes who strained to uphold God's law in the city of his great temple. But the whole purpose of God's law was to prepare his people to receive his King, and the whole point of God's temple was to demonstrate God's willingness to dwell with mankind, a willingness brought to fulfillment when God came in the person of his Son.

The Pharisees and scribes couldn't see that by rejecting Jesus they were distancing themselves from God's wings of refuge and heading toward eternal separation from his goodness. When they said "no" to Jesus, they lost everything they thought they had.

If you're wondering whether the cost of standing out from the crowd is worth paying, it's vital to recognize this warning: If you stay away from Jesus, you won't be able to hold on to what you currently have—and you won't ever attain what you truly want.

BLESSED ARE THE PEOPLE OF THE SON

Helen Shapiro is a Jewish singer who was a household name in Britain in the early 1960s, with five hits reaching the top 10 of the British charts, and two number ones. Not many singers can say, as she can, that they once headlined a concert featuring The Beatles as a warm-up act. In the 1980s, Helen began exploring Jesus's claim to be the Jewish Messiah until she reached the point when, in her words, "I believed that Jesus was the Messiah, the Son of God and God the Son. I believed that he died on the cross, was buried and rose from the dead on the third day." Given her fame in the Jewish community, it's no surprise that she says, "This was controversial!"[12]

12 Helen's story can be read at www.jewishtestimonies.com.

These lines, taken from one of the Gospel songs Helen now sings, capture something of the joy of gathering beneath Jesus's wings, despite the pain of no longer blending in with the crowd:

> Born in a world full of sorrow,
> Spoke of a better world yet to come,
> Words of hope and of promise—
> Blessed are the people who know the Son,
> Blessed are the people who know the Son.[13]

Do you know this blessing? As we can tell from the example of the leaders Jesus spoke to, it's possible to be outwardly respectable, to have impressive Bible knowledge, and to be familiar with the things of God, while all the time keeping away from Jesus himself. He wants to gather you to him as a hen gathers her chicks beneath her wings. Will you be gathered to him?

---

13 From "Blessed Are the People," on Helen's album *What Wondrous Love Is This.*

TGC | THE **GOSPEL** COALITION

The Gospel Coalition is a fellowship of evangelical churches deeply committed to renewing our faith in the gospel of Christ and to reforming our ministry practices to conform fully to the Scriptures. We have committed ourselves to invigorating churches with new hope and compelling joy based on the promises received by grace alone through faith alone in Christ alone.

We desire to champion the gospel with clarity, compassion, courage, and joy—gladly linking hearts with fellow believers across denominational, ethnic, and class lines. We yearn to work with all who, in addition to embracing our confession and theological vision for ministry, seek the lordship of Christ over the whole of life with unabashed hope in the power of the Holy Spirit to transform individuals, communities, and cultures.

Join the cause and visit TGC.org for fresh resources that will equip you to love God with all your heart, soul, mind, and strength, and to love your neighbor as yourself.

T G C . O R G